A Gardener's Guide To Weeds

How To Use Common Garden Weeds For Food, Health, Beauty And More

Jason Johns

Visit me at www.GardeningWithJason.com for gardening tips and advice or follow me at www.YouTube.com/OwningAnAllotment for my video diary and tips. Join me on Facebook at www.Facebook.com/OwningAnAllotment.

Follow me on Instagram and Twitter as @allotmentowner for regular updates, tips and to ask your gardening questions.

If you have enjoyed this book, please leave a review on Amazon. I read each review personally and the feedback helps me to continually improve my books.

TABLE OF CONTENTS

What Makes A Weed? 1

How Weeds Can Be Beneficial 4

Making Weed Concoctions 8

Weed Directory 14

Bittercress...15

Broad Leaf Dock 18

Chickweed 24

Cleavers..28

Clover (Red & White) 32

Coltsfoot 40

Comfrey..44

Common Plantain 48

Couch Grass..53

Crow Garlic 56

Dandelion 58

Elderberry 66

Fat Hen 72

Field Milk Thistle..76

Field Pennycress..79

Ground Elder...82

Himalayan Balsam 85

Jewelweed 89

Kudzu 92

Mallow 98

Mare's Tail / Horsetail 101

Mullien 106

Nettles 109

Purple Deadnettle 116

Purslane 120

Rosebay Willowherb 124

Self-Heal 128

Shepherd's Purse 132

Wood Sorrel 136

Yarrow 140

Endnote 144

About Jason 147

Other Books By Jason 149

Want More Inspiring Gardening Ideas? 157

WHAT MAKES A WEED?

Everyone looks at a plant in the garden one day and asks themselves, "Is that a weed?", particularly in spring when everything is starting to grow.

But what is a weed?

If a rose planted started to grow in my herb garden, then it is a weed because it is not meant to be there. If garlic or celery self-seeds and starts to grow in my flower garden, then they are weeds as they are not meant to be there.

A weed is simply a plant that is not wanted in the place it has decided to grow. As we try to bring order to the chaos that is nature, we want to control which plants grow well to please us aesthetically.

We all look at plants that are growing out of place in our gardens and think they are weeds, but they are purely misplaced plants. Mare's tail or dandelions growing in between our neatly ordered rows of carrots are a prime example of weeds. We don't want them there, that's where the carrots grow in our sense of order of things.

What you may not realize, is that all those plants you are pulling up and composting while getting annoyed at them for daring to infringe on your growing area, are actually useful plants that we have forgotten how to use! Many of these plants can be eaten or have medicinal uses, but they have fallen out of favor as fewer people grow plants and more people buy whatever the supermarket has on offer.

Many of these plants have significant health benefits, but as well as that, they are tasty too! They often are not as sweet as plants we are used to eating from stores, but over the last 40-50 years, our palates have changed and we are now less used to the natural, bitter taste of many greens, preferring sweeter tasting plants.

This book will introduce you to many of the weeds that are growing in your garden, probably ones you are pulling up and getting annoyed about. This is your opportunity to get your revenge on these weeds and start to use them to benefit you! So instead of feeling frustrated when you see a weed peeking its head up in between your vegetable plants, you will feel a sense of elation because you know it is a useful plant that benefits you!

For me, this completely changes the approach to gardening as you stop being so militant about many of the weeds growing in your garden. This doesn't mean you allow them to grow unchecked and out of control. It means that you allow the weeds to grow large enough for them to be useful to you, and then you remove them and put them to good use.

You will be surprised by just how many 'weeds' are actually really useful plants that can benefit you in many ways. Just remember, that herbal medicines should not be used as a substitute for professional medical advice and that if you are undergoing any treatment or taking any medication, you should always speak to a qualified doctor before taking herbs as medicines.

Enjoy finding out more about the weeds that are growing in your garden and how you can use them to benefit you! It is time to stop the weed wars and start benefiting from these free plants!

How Weeds Can Be Beneficial

When a weed appears in our neatly ordered world of rows of vegetables, it upsets our sense of order and we have to get rid of it. While it is okay to get rid of weeds in your vegetable garden, many of these weeds are useful. As you read this book, you will find out which of these herbs you can eat and what medicinal uses they have, plus much of the native wildlife rely on weeds to live and/or feed on. Nettles, for example, are home to several species of butterfly whose caterpillars rely on them for food.

It is okay for weeds to grow in your garden and they

can be really, really helpful. If you don't want them to spread uncontrollably, after they have flowered, dead-head them to stop them from going to seed!

But weeds also have a use beyond this and are surprisingly beneficial for us all:

- Feeding Bees – many weeds flower and these usually cover most of the year, providing valuable food sources for bees and other insects. I allow dandelions to flower in my garden as they are a vital early season food source for bees. Once the flowers are spent, I remove them to prevent the seeds from spreading. I let most weeds flower to attract pollinators into my vegetable garden and help them as in most urban areas, they can struggle for food.

- Preventing Erosion – areas with heavy rain, high winds or sloping hills can suffer from erosion of topsoil. When these areas are stripped bare of weeds, then the topsoil erodes, leaving behind a dead soil that nothing grows in. Weeds hold the soil in place and prevent erosion from occurring. They are great on built up banks and exposed areas to protect the soil.

- As a Mulch – during hot weather, weeds help keep the soil cool and prevent plants from bolting. They can help to lock moisture into the soil and protect the beneficial micro-organisms and life in the soil.

- Breaking Up Soil – weeds with long tap roots like thistles, docks and dandelions are great at breaking up compacted soil. While some people plant tillage radishes or mooli, you can allow these plants to grow for the same effect. In order for the root to die and break up the soil, you will need to regularly chop the plants to the ground, but they work just as effectively.

- Soil Health Indicator – weeds can tell you the

quality and type of soil in your garden, once you know how to read them. If lamb's quarters grows tall, then it shows that your soil is high in nitrogen, but if it is stunted, then your soil is low in nitrogen. Crabgrass shows your soil is dry and compacted. If everything except crabgrass is struggling to grow, your soil is likely low in calcium. These are good indicators of the condition of your soil and can help you know what will grow well in it.

- Indicates Soil Depth – weeds with tap roots indicate how deep your top soil is. If dandelions, docks, lamb's quarters and other weeds grow shallow, sprawling root systems, then you know that the nutrients and water is in the top few inches of soil. If they are really long and go deep, then you know you have good quality, deep soil. This influences what you plan as shallow rooted plants can go in the shallow areas of soil and deep rooted plants can go in the deeper areas.

- Fixing Nitrogen – some weeds, such as clover, takes nitrogen from the air and stores it in nodes on their roots. When the plant dies and the roots rot down, this nitrogen becomes available for other plants. However, clover needs to die before it flowers for the nitrogen to be useful. So allow the clover to grow and then just before it flowers, cut it down, rip out the roots and dig them into the soil. You are using naturally occurring clover as a green manure to benefit your soil.

- Bio-accumulators – certain weeds are excellent at extracting minerals from the soil that other plants may struggle to access. Plants such as ragweed, can access minerals over a wide range of pH levels and have complex root systems that allow them to collect minerals. Let these plants grow and before they flower, dig them up and compost them so that the minerals become bioavailable, i.e. accessible by other plants.

- Plant Food – some weeds, such as nettle and comfrey, make for excellent plant feeds if you cut them back and prepare them before they seed

- Great Compost – most weeds are great on your compost heap and can be used as 'green' material in the composting process. Weeds that spread from their roots, such as mare's tail and bindweed, can be left to dry and then added to your compost as 'brown' material.

- Livestock Feed – livestock such as goats, pigs and chickens will eat many weeds. Goats will eat pretty much anything, but chickens are a little bit more sensitive and certain plants aren't good for them. However, if you keep chickens, you will be aware of this and know that well-fed chickens keep away from these harmful plants.

Making Weed Concoctions

These are simple techniques for how to use the weeds in your garden medicinally and for beauty purposes. These the basic ways of using the plants detailed in the next section, though each plant may be used in multiple ways. All of these can be made with a single plant or, if you want to combine effects from different weeds, multiple weeds can be used.

Decoction

A decoction is similar to a herbal tea, made by boiling plant matter in water. Decoctions have a very long history but have fallen out of favor somewhat today, mainly because it is an older style drink and takes a bit longer than a tea to make.

A basic decoction is made like this:

1. Use 1 teaspoon or tablespoon (depending on the strength required) of plant material per cup of water
2. Add the plant and water to a saucepan
3. Bring to a gentle boil
4. Cover, a simmer lightly for between 20 and 40

minutes

5. Remove from the heat and allow to cool to drinking temperature

6. Strain the solid matter from the drink, sweeten if required and enjoy

Any leftover liquid can be refrigerated and used in the next day or two. Usually, you can use the same plants a couple of times for this, providing the decoction is still strong enough. Once you have finished, the plant material can be composted.

It is always best to start with cold water, rather than putting the plants directly into boiling water. When any plants are placed in hot water, the albumen in the plant cells bind, which makes it very hard to get the beneficial constituents of the plant into the water.

Fresh or dried plant material can be used to make a decoction. Supermarket bought dried herbs will work for a decoction, particularly if you want to add mint to some weeds for a bit of flavor. As fresh herbs have a high water content, always use double the amount of fresh herbs compared to dried herbs.

Some people prefer to grind or crush the plant matter before boiling them. This increases the surface area of the plant and makes it easier to get the beneficial constituents out of the plant.

Covering the pan while simmering is very important as many of the beneficial oils in a plant will evaporate off in the heat. The lid keeps these constituents in the pan and helps to concentrate them. If the plant is high in volatile oils, boil the woody parts of it and then add the leaves when you remove the pan from the heat. Keep the pan covered and this will prevent the volatile oils escaping and being lost. Herbs high in volatile oils include fennel, peppermint and valerian.

Infusion or Tea

An infusion is very simply a herbal tea, it is nothing more

complex! Infusions are usually made with leaves and flowers, but roots and seeds are used when boiling would lose volatile oils. Seeds and roots are best slightly crushed before infusing so that the water can get to the constituents inside the harder, outer shell.

Both fresh and dried plant material can be used, though adjust quantities as required for the strength infusion you prefer. Infusions can be drunk or used as a hair rinse or skin toner, depending on the plant it is made from.

Use one to two teaspoons of the dried plant per cup of water, or three teaspoons of fresh plant. Put the plant material into a cup, ideally using a strainer or tea ball, though you can put them in loose. I use a coffee cafetiere for my infusions as it is simple to use and saves straining the plant out later on.

Once the infusion has steeped for 10 to 20 minutes, depending on how strong you want it, then strain off the plant material and drink. Cover the infusion while it is steeping to prevent volatile oils escaping.

Infusions are best drunk immediately or turned into an iced tea. They will keep for a day or two in your refrigerator.

Infused Oil

Infused oils can be used for beauty or culinary purposes and can be made from any light oil. Most people use extra-virgin olive oil, but any other oil will work such as rapeseed oil or sunflower oil.

It is best to use fresh plant material for an infused oil. Leave them to wilt for 12-24 hours by arranging them in a single layer on kitchen paper before infusing them. This removes some of the water content from the plant and prevents the oil from going moldy or spoiling. You can dry the plant fully first if you prefer and have time.

Quarter fill a heat proof jar with the plant material, crumbling it a little as you do. Slowly fill the jar with your choice of oil until the jar is mostly full; best to leave some headroom. Stir the contents of the jar well, seal and leave somewhere cool and dark for between 4-6 weeks. You can then strain the solid matter from the oil and store the infused oil in a dark glass container in a cool, dark place.

Infused oils can be made faster by heating the jar in a double boiler for a few hours, though you need to be careful not to burn or overheat it.

Poultice

Poultices have been used for thousands of years and are a very good way to use plants on your skin and harness their healing properties, particularly wound healers like yarrow. They allow you to enjoy the benefits of weeds without the concentration of a tincture or essential oil.

A poultice is a paste made from weeds mixed with anything from salts to clays to activated charcoal or a whole host of other, beneficial substances. However, you can just mix the plants with water and use this, it has been effective for thousands of years! This is then wrapped in cloth and placed on your skin. It can then be covered with a waterproof covering and left on your skin for several hours. The poultice is changed regularly throughout the day.

A poultice can be made with fresh or dried plant material, depending on what you have available. The important thing is that the plant material is in contact with the skin. Poultices are used for anything from boils to burns to splinters and more.

A poultice should not be a substitute for medical treatment, but can be used to assist medical treatment. Make sure you tell your doctor that you are going to use a herbal poultice in case there is any interaction between the plants you use and any prescription drugs you may be taking.

A poultice is made with water. Hot water is used when a poultice is trying to draw something out from a person, while cold water is used to bring down inflammation. Traditionally, a mortar and pestle is used to crush plants for a poultice, but these days, people are just as likely to use a food processor or blender. Ground dried herbs, such as those bought from a supermarket, can be used in addition to the weeds.

Adding a little bit of hot water to any poultice, directly to the plant can assist the healing process as it will help to extract the beneficial constituents of the herbs. Then use hot/cold water to get a temperature that is comfortable for your skin and apply it.

You are aiming to create a thick paste that can be directly applied to the skin or wrapped in a clean cloth and applied. Cheesecloth works very well for this, though you can use any cloth that does not absorb a lot of liquid or is too thick for the plants to come into contact with the skin.

A simple poultice is made for two or three tablespoons of plant material ground down and mixed with hot or cold water to form a paste. Healing clays or activated charcoal can be added, depending on what you are treating. This is then cooled to room temperature (if hot) before applying, or applying directly if cold water was used. Depending on the plants used, you can wrap the poultice in cheesecloth and then use a waterproof covering such as kitchen plastic wrap, to keep the poultice in place.

Leave it on the skin for anywhere from 20 minutes to up to three hours, repeating as needed.

Poultices can be made out of almost any herb or weed, though with some you need to be careful not to apply the plant matter directly to the skin. A poultice made out of common plantain, which grows freely as a weed virtually everywhere is excellent to heal insect bites and bee stings. Cabbage leaf poultices are good for treating mastitis and a fresh garlic poultice is said to cure warts!

Tincture

Tinctures are infusions made with alcohol. They store well, usually for at least a year in a dark bottle in cool, dark place. These can be used as is or mixed with other oils or creams to make beauty products.

A tincture of lemon balm is made by filling a jar three quarters full with fresh, washed leaves. Fill the jar with an 80% proof alcohol such as vodka, seal and leave in a cool, dark place for between four and six weeks, shaking occasionally. Strain and then store for up to a year.

This tincture, like many others, is taken at a dose of ¼ teaspoon or 1ml at a time. It is not recommended for children. Mix with honey to make it more palatable.

Glycerite

A glycerite is similar to a tincture but doesn't contain any alcohol. They are used as ingredients in many beauty products such as toners, aftershave and lotions.

A glycerite can be made from lemon balm very easily. Fill a jar with freshly washed lemon balm leaves. Cover the leaves with a mixture of three parts vegetable glycerine to one part water. Seal and leave in a cool, dark place for three to four weeks. Strain and then store in a dark bottle in your refrigerator for several months. The adult dosage is ½ to 1 teaspoon as required to help you relax and stay calm.

Herbal Vinegar

Herbal vinegars have many uses at home, from beauty uses such as hair rinses and bath additives to use in the kitchen as salad dressings.

Lemon balm makes an excellent vinegar and is easily made. Fill a jar ¾ full with freshly washed lemon balm leaves. Cover it with apple cider vinegar. Seal and leave in a cool, dark place for four to six weeks. Strain and then use as required. This will store in a dark glass bottle for 9 to 12 months or even longer.

WEED DIRECTORY

This section lists many of the weeds commonly found in your garden. You will learn all about the weed and discover how it can be of use to you! When I first started looking into this, I was shocked to find just how many of the 'weeds' in my garden were good to eat or had medicinal uses. It is a real eye opener to see how many of these plants have fallen out of favor today, yet in the past were a staple food!

Many of these plants can even be found sold as dried herbs. I remember finding mare's tail for sale in a shop and thinking that I could supply them with the amount I had growing! Many herbalists cultivate these weeds and many people interested in herbalism buy these weeds, fresh or dried, to use at home. If you are not interested in using them yourself, I am sure you can find someone locally who would be happy to trade with you for them.

BITTERCRESS

Hairy bittercress, *Cardamine hirsute*, is a common weed that is a member of the mustard family (*Brassicaceae*) that grows substantially in a year! Native to both Europe and Asia, it is a biennial or winter annual (dies off in the cold), but it has spread across the globe and is now found pretty much everywhere. It is also known as 'flickweed' as when the seeds are ripe, the pods flick them out. In the New Forest, England, it has the local name of 'Jumping Jesus' for the same reason. The plant typically has a twelve-week lifecycle.

Hairy bittercress in flower and with seed pods

It is noticeable by a dense rosette of leaves and many erect stems that look like those found on other mustards. The seed pods grow along the upper stem, below the flower but above the leaves. The white flowers are small, no bigger than 5mm long and have four petals, growing in small clusters at the top of each vertical stem. The flowers will typically appear anytime from April through to June, depending on where you live. The kidney shaped leaves alternate on the stems and the stalk is slightly hairy.

Hairy bittercress grows up to 12"/30cm tall, preferring bare soil in woodlands or lightly grassed areas. It grows well on dry slopes, forest margins, wasteland, rocky outcrops and, of course, in your garden where it will spread rapidly as the seed pods explode when you try to pull the weed up.

Gardening Uses

This plant doesn't really have any uses in the garden except to be composted. It can spread very rapidly in any garden due to its explosive seed mechanism. It's relative, wavy bittercress (*Cardamine fluexuosa*) grows much larger, sometimes as much as 18"/50cm compared to hairy bittercress which is often only a few inches tall.

Culinary Uses

This is a great plant to use when you would normally use uncooked cress such as pestos, salsa and salad. When you cook it, the arugula (rocket) flavor comes out. Both the flowers and leaves are edible, though the flowers can be a little tough to chew.

Bittercress Pesto

This is how you make pesto from bittercress. The original recipe from Genoa did not use pine nuts, but feel free to add them to this if you like.

Ingredients:
- 15 hairy bittercress rosettes
- 1 garlic clove
- 2-3 tablespoons extra-virgin olive oil
- ½ teaspoon sugar
- Squeeze of lemon juice
- Salt and pepper to taste

Method:
1. Cut the bottom of the bittercress rosettes off (root area), then rinse the leaves well, leaving to drain in a colander
2. Heat a frying pan and cook the garlic clove for a couple of minutes to help reduce its pungency
3. Put all of the ingredients into your blender with half the olive oil and blend using short bursts
4. Add more olive oil until you reach the thickness and texture you desire

Medicinal Uses
The leaves are tender and are packed with antioxidants, vitamin C, beta-carotene, calcium and vitamin C, which all act to boost your immune system.

Folklore Myth and Legend
There is little folklore associated with this plant. In some areas of England, it is known as Jumping Jesus due to its explosive seed pods. It is well known to gardeners due to its rapid growth and spread over vegetable beds.

BROAD LEAF DOCK

Dock, *Rumex obtusifolius*, is the bane of many a gardener when it gets established. It can grow up to 20-51"/50-130cm tall and the same down into the ground, or at least that is how it feels. It is very easy to recognize with its oval leaves that can grow up to 16"/40cm long and used to counteract nettle stings.

The plant produces long flower stalks from June to September, which should be removed by the gardener before it can disperse its seeds. These turn brown as the seeds ripen, and the seeds disperse over late fall to early winter, sometimes remaining in place throughout winter. Each plant can produce thousands of seeds which will quickly take root.

Curly dock, *Rumex crispus*, is similar in appearance, but has thinner, wavier leaves and is commonly referred to as yellow dock. Other edible docks include western dock (*Rumex occidentalis*), yard dock (*Rumex longifolius*) and field dock (*Rumex stenphyllus*). Wild rhubarb (*Rumex hymenosepalus*) is common in the deserts of Southwest America and is larger and more succulent that its relatives. Wild rhubarb is a traditional food of some Native American tribes and can also be used as a dye.

One type of dock is sometimes cultivated, patience dock (*Rumex patientia*). Seeds can still be found online for it, though sometimes it can be found in the wild. It is a larger, more tender plant with more flavor than other dock plants.

Gardening Uses
Apart from adding the leaves to your compost bin, there are no real gardening uses for this plant. The long roots can be helpful in breaking up hard soil, but they grow very deep and can be difficult to remove. This plant will grow back from any bits of root left in the soil, making it a tough plant to get rid of when established. It is advisable to remove this plant as soon as you see a seedling so it does not get the chance to establish itself.

The established plants can be cut down before they set seed. The woody stalks can be dried and make for an excellent kindling.

Culinary Uses
Dock leaves can be used in a salad, cooked like spinach or used to prepare a vegetable broth. They contain a substance called oxalic acid, which can be unpleasant to you if you eat too much. Oxalic acid is also found in spinach, so if you have been told not to eat spinach, you should also avoid dock. The dried seeds are used as a spice or ground into a flour as the plant is a distant relative of buckwheat.

During the Great Depression, docks were a popular plant to eat as they were abundant and have a tart, lemony flavor.

Docks has a thin sheath covering the nodes where the leaves emerge, known as the 'ocrea'. As the plant ages, this turns brown, so the condition of the ocrea gives you an idea of the age and tenderness of the leaves.

The best leaves come from young docks that haven't yet developed flower stalks. These leaves tend to be more tender and have more flavor. Pick two to six of the youngest leaves from the middle of each clump. It doesn't matter if they haven't unfurled and they are likely to still be mucilaginous.

In early to mid-spring, the young leaves can be eaten raw or cooked. When eating raw, remove the leaf stem (petiole) and only use the leaves to avoid consuming too much mucilage. The midribs on larger leaves can be quite tough and so should be removed before eating. The petioles can be cut into smaller pieces and used instead of rhubarb.

Boil or sauté docks to get the best flavor from them, though they are good in a wide variety of dishes from soups to stews to stir-fries and egg dishes. Cooked dock works surprisingly well with dairy and is excellent mixed with cream cheese.

As the harvesting season for dock is relatively short, you can blanch and freeze the leaves for use out of season.

Dock in flower

Yorkshire Dock Pudding Recipe
This is a traditional recipe in Yorkshire, England, originating in the Calder Valley where they hold a World Dock Pudding Competition every year. It doesn't use traditional dock leaves, but a variety known as common bistort, *Persicaria Bistorta*, which can be found growing in the wild or cultivated. It also makes use of stinging nettles and the resulting pudding has a taste somewhere between asparagus and spinach. It works surprisingly well when served with bacon dishes!

Ingredients:
- 2lb/900g young common bistort leaves (remove large veins and stalks)
- 8oz/225g young nettle tops
- 2 onions (finely chopped)
- 3 tablespoons oatmeal
- Small knob of butter

Method:
1. Wash both sets of leaves and strain
2. Put the leaves and onions in a pan with some

salted water and boil until tender

3. Add the oatmeal, stir well and simmer for 20 minutes
4. Strain off excess liquid
5. Add the butter and stir well until melted
6. Season to taste with salt and pepper
7. Fry the resulting pudding, ideally in bacon fat

Stuffed Dock Leaves

This method of serving dock is popular in Turkey and surrounding areas and is reminiscent of the Greek stuffed vine leaves. They are a popular 'wild' food across most of Europe and can be stuffed with pretty much anything you want. Folding them is probably the hardest part of this and how you do it will depend on the size of the dock leaves. It won't take you long though to do it well.

Ingredients:
- 8 dock leaves (thoroughly washed)
- 9oz/250g lamb/beef/plant based mince
- 2oz/50g bulgur wheat
- ½ pint/200ml cold water
- ½ onion (finely chopped)
- 1 large tomato (finely chopped)
- Juice of 1 lemon
- 2 tablespoons walnut oil
- 1 tablespoon tomato purée
- 4 teaspoons Parmesan cheese (grated)
- ½ teaspoon mixed spices

Method:
1. Preheat your oven to 350F/180C
2. Boil the dock leaves for a couple of minutes in water, then drain, and boil again
3. Drain the dock leaves and pat dry with kitchen paper

23

4. In a bowl, stir together 1 tablespoon of walnut oil with the mince, lemon juice, onion, bulgur wheat, mixed spice and tomato until thoroughly combined (add a little water to loosen the mixture up if necessary)
5. Roll this mixture into 8 balls of the same size
6. Wrap each ball in a dock leaf
7. Put the stuffed leaves into a saucepan or cast-iron casserole dish
8. Mix the rest of the oil with the water and tomato purée, then pour over the stuffed dock leaves
9. Put the dish on your hob and heat on a medium heat until the liquid starts to boil
10. Remove the dish from the heat and transfer to your oven
11. Cook for 30 minutes then cool slightly before serving
12. Grate the cheese over the stuffed dock leaves before serving

Medicinal Uses

The best known use for dock, which many of us learn as children, is to treat nettle stings. Fortuitously, dock and nettle grow in very similar soil conditions and are usually found close by each other. Because of this soothing ability, dock leaves are also used to treat burns, scalds and blisters.

The root is very high in tannin and has astringent properties. The root is made into a tea which is used to treat a variety of conditions from jaundice to boils to whooping cough. In an infusion, the root is an excellent wash to treat skin eruptions. The root is best harvested early spring time and dried to use later in the year.

As the leaves contain oxalic acid, people who suffer from kidney stones, gout, arthritis or hyperacidity should avoid eating dock as it can aggravate their condition.

Folklore, Myths and Legends

Dock is probably best known for its ability to ease nettle stings. Whether it does or does not is still a matter of debate, but it certainly does make you feel better about a nettle sting.

One piece of folklore associated with the dock is that it was smoked by the Native Americans and called Indian Tobacco. This is not true and was a misunderstanding many years ago caused by the Alnwick Garden Poison Garden. Indian Tobacco is Lobelia inflate which does look similar to dock, but certainly is not the same plant.

CHICKWEED

Common chickweed, *Stellaria media*, has hairless leaves with a single row of hairs on the stems and is commonly referred to as stitchwort. Mouse-ear chickweed, *Cerastium fontanum*, is virtually identical, but has fuzzy leaves. Both are mat-forming plants from the *Caryophyllaceae* family and occur natively in a lot of countries across the world. It is a short-lived perennial with a long taproot and nodal rooted branches that sprawl over a large area. This plant is commonly found in vegetable gardens where it spreads out over a relatively large area of ground, crowding out other weeds, but is relatively simple to remove.

Chickweed flowers from early to mid-spring, producing small, white flowers with a split at the tip of every petal. The flowers are around 1cm across and have five white petals with ten stamens.

Chickweed can grow as high as 1½ feet/50cm tall, though the stems are rarely erect and the plant sprawls along the ground. Roots will form at the nodes, so you have to be a bit more diligent when removing it.

This weed is very common, often seen taking over your lawn, but can be found in a many other locations, including fields, wasteland and even on the forest floor.

Gardening Uses

Chickweed is a good sign of good quality soil as it grows in fertile soil. It can also indicate low calcium or phosphorous and can also indicate high levels of potassium in the soil.

Culinary Uses

The leaves are eaten raw in sandwiches or salads, but can be added to stews and soups. When cooking, the stems and flowers can also be used, but if you are eating this raw, then only the leaves are used.

Buttered Chickweed
The combination of onions and chickweed really works in this dish, which is great on the side of a main meal. It takes about 10 minutes to make and serves two people.

Ingredients:
- 2 cups chickweed leaves (chopped)
- 1 onion (finely chopped)

- Butter
- Salt and pepper to taste

Method:
1. Wash the chickweed thoroughly
2. Boil a pan of salted water
3. Add the chickweed and cook for 2-3 minutes
4. Drain well (note that the liquid can be used as a chickweed tea)
5. Melt some butter in a frying pan
6. Sauté the onion until translucent
7. Add the chickweed and season to taste
8. Sauté for a further minute before serving

Medicinal Uses
Chickweed has been used by humans for thousands of years. Evidence has been found at pre-Neolithic sites in Britain that early humans were using his plant. Having spread throughout the world, it was extensively used by Native American tribes for treating complaints including coughs, colds, flu, sore throats and other respiratory disorders.

In Europe, it was used to treat indigestion, bronchitis and asthma. Due to its high levels of vitamin C, sailors made a concoction called 'chickweed vinegar' that they drank on long voyages to prevent scurvy.

Chickweed also contains saponins which help to ease inflamed mucous membranes and break up their secretions. It is both an expectorant and a demulcent, helping both to ease lung congestion and clear mucous. These saponins also help to emulsify fat cells and expel them from the body as well as generally improving the health of a digestive tract. Chickweed contains lecithin, which aids fat metabolism and the herb is naturally an appetite suppressant. It also supports a healthy thyroid system. Chickweed is also a mild laxative and diuretic, which helps the body flush toxins from its system.

Chickweed was used to help draw out splinters and then heal the wound, but is mostly known for its healing effect on wounds and bites.

Folklore, Myths and Legends

In Europe, it was used to attract love, maintain relationships and ensure fidelity. A sprig of chickweed was carried to ensure one's partner was faithful and to draw the attention of a loved one.

Culpeper, the famous 17th century herbalist, believed chickweed to be under the rule of the moon and was associated with feminine energies as well as love and fertility. It was a common ingredient in love potions.

CLEAVERS

Cleavers, *Galium aparine*, is a member of the *Rubiaceae* family, which contains flowering plants in the bedstraw and coffee family. Cleavers, or burdock bestraw as it is known in some areas, is best known for its ability to stick to literally anything from clothing to pets and its little sticky balls that are difficult to remove. It is also, unsurprisingly, known as sticky bud or sticky weed, with few people knowing it is actually called cleavers. It is also known by the names sticky willie and goosegrass.

Be aware that some people can develop a rash from touching this plant. If you do, then do not, under any circumstances, eat or use this plant.

Cleavers is an annual plant that creeps along the ground or climbs up through other plants. It can often be seen leaning out of a hedgerow, its sticky branches reaching out to attach themselves to any passing human or animal. It can grow up to 6 feet/2 meters in length and take over an area very quickly. Fortunately, it is easy to remove as it has shallow roots.

This plant does flower, though the flowers are so small (1-2mm in size) that they are rarely noticed. Consisting of four small white petals arranged in clusters of up to nine flowers on side branches, these appear from late spring through to summer.

The narrow leaves form at the stem joints in groups of between six and nine. The lance shaped leaves are covered in tiny hooked hairs, designed to catch onto animal fur and now human clothing.

Cleavers grows in hedgerows, overgrown gardens or on the edges of fields. It can be found growing pretty much anywhere as it is very adaptable. Native to Europe and western Asia, it has spread across the world and is now common in most temperate areas and even in some sub-tropical areas.

Gardening Uses

As an invasive plant that will do its best to choke out other plants, it is not cultivated by gardeners, but will appear in the vegetable garden as a weed. The plant can be composted, though best not to compost the seeds unless you are hot composting.

Culinary Uses

While cleavers is best known for its medicinal uses, the leaves and stems can be used like any other leaf vegetable. The stickiness of the leaves means it does not work very well in salads, but it can be sautéed. The little round sticky balls that form the fruit of this plant can be roasted and then used as a coffee substitute. Both the leaves and stems can be dried and used to make a tea.

The tea is made by adding 2-3 teaspoons of the herb to a cup of boiling water and infusing for 10-15 minutes. Drink 2-3 cups of cleavers tea per day to benefit from this plant.

Cleavers and Eggplant Bake
This is a nice bake that uses the tips of the cleavers plant to add flavor. Try to pick the younger tips from higher up to avoid contamination.

Ingredients:
- 23oz/650g eggplant (aubergine – sliced)
- 5¼oz/150g cleavers tips
- 2 onions (sliced)
- 2 garlic cloves (chopped)
- 1 tin chopped tomatoes
- 17½fl oz/500ml cheese sauce
- 2 tablespoons mixed herbs
- 2 teaspoons tomato puree
- Salt to taste

Method:
1. Slice the eggplant and lightly oil each slice
2. Grill on a high heat for 2 minutes, turning occasionally, until wilted
3. Wash the cleavers and then, without shaking it dry, fry it in a pan then put to one side
4. Sauté the garlic and onions for a few minutes until translucent
5. Add the tin of tomatoes, tomato puree, a pinch of salt and the mixed herbs, stirring well
6. Simmer for 15 minutes
7. Make the cheese sauce
8. Layer a dish with tomato sauce, eggplant, cleavers and cheese sauce until all of the ingredients are used up, ending with a layer of cheese sauce
9. Bake at 400F/200C for about 30 minutes until piping hot and bubbling

Medicinal Uses

Cleavers has been long used in both Chinese and European medicine. In Chinese medicine, it is used to disperse stagnancy and inflammation and to treat urinary problems. It is an excellent first aid herb and is good for treating skin problems and flushing the lymphatic system and kidneys.

As a natural diuretic, it flushes the kidneys and the urinary tract, so is excellent for treating urinary infections and cystitis. It can help relieve water retention and has been used to treat ulcers, tumors and lumps in the breast.

Externally, cleavers has a number of uses too due to its antiseptic and astringent properties. It is a good herb for healing wounds and calming skin irritations of any type. It is used to treat boils and abscesses as well as dermatitis, psoriasis and eczema. Cleavers is also useful in treating sunburn, wounds and burns.

Folklore, Myths and Legends

There is no known folklore associated with this plant, though children still enjoy throwing this sticky plant at each other. In the past, the root was used to create a red dye and the sticky buds were used by lace makers to enlarge pinheads.

Jason Johns

CLOVER (RED & WHITE)

Clover grows in the wild and is a member of the legume family, commonly used as cattle food. The two most common types of clover are red (*Trifolium pratense*) and white (*Trifolium repens*). Red clover is the most commonly used of the two. White clover flowers can still be eaten like red clover, but the leaves are unpalatable even when cooked. Red clover has the most medicinal uses whereas white clover has fewer, but still contains plenty of vitamins and minerals.

Clover is very recognizable plant that almost everyone is familiar with. Many of us spent time as children looking for the genetic mutation of the clover that is considered lucky … the four leaf clover. In the past, this hunt was used to distract children and keep them quiet while the parents enjoyed a picnic or day out.

The flowers grow to about an inch (2-3cm) across and

are made up of lots of tiny, tubular shaped flowers. If you look closely, you will see each flower has five narrow petals that are usually pink or purple/pink and becoming lighter or white as they get closer to the base of the flower. Flowers appear from mid to late spring and, depending on the weather conditions, continue to bloom until late October.

Many people think of clover has being a low growing plant, but that tends to be because we see it on lawns that are mowed, so it has adapted. Red clover in particular can grow to about 2½ feet/80cm tall in the right conditions.

Clover will grow almost anywhere and is a common site in empty lots, grassy verges and fields. It is the bane of many home owners, being more than happy to grow in the middle of your lawn! It can be difficult to get rid of as it spreads rapidly, but it is easy enough to pull up and remove.

White clover

Clover is used by some gardeners as a green manure, where it is grown and then dug into the soil before the flowers finish. As a green manure, clover is excellent at fixing nitrogen into the soil, improving the soil structure and keeping down other weeds as it grows so quickly, providing the roots are dug into the soil. The flowers are extremely beneficial to bees, and many gardeners will plant this purely to feed bees and then dig it into the ground over winter.

The ancient druids believed clover warded off evil and in particular, witches. The Medieval Christians associated the three lobed leaves with the Holy Trinity while the four leaf clovers were symbolic of the cross.

Gardening Uses

Clover is good in a garden to help distract rabbits from the plants you are cultivating. Of course, you can eat it both raw or cooked or use it to make a herbal tea.

Clover attracts earthworms into your garden and is an excellent soil fertilizer as it pulls nitrogen out of the air and locks it into the soil. Rather than pull clover up, dig it into the ground and let it naturally break down to benefit from this nitrogen. Clover can also be used as a green manure and can be put on the compost heap.

Culinary Uses

While you can eat the leaves of the clover plant in a salad, or make it into a tea, the flowers are more commonly eaten. As the clover is related to the pea, the leaves do have a slightly bean flavor. As well as being eaten raw, the leaves are used in soups, stews and dishes like lasagna.

However, it is not recommended to eat too many red clover flowers as some people feel bloated afterwards.

Make sure you harvest the flowers before they start to turn brown. They can be used raw in salads or sautéed.

Dried, they make for a lovely tea or can be ground up to make a flour substitute.

The roots are edible, but should always be cooked first.

Both the leaves and flowers can be harvested and dried for use throughout the winter.

White Clover Pudding
Clover is a member of the legume family and white clover is high in protein, nutrients and minerals. The flowers can even be turned into a flour, which is used in baking.

Ingredients:
- 2 cups white clover blossoms (discard brown petals and remove the petals from the flower head)
- 1 cup water
- 1 cup heavy (double) cream (whipped to stiffness)
- ½ cup fresh squeezed orange juice
- 4 tablespoons honey (white clover honey is best if you can find it)
- 1 tablespoon unflavored gelatin
- Pinch of salt

Method:
1. Dissolve the gelatin into ¼ cup of water
2. In a small saucepan, bring the clover flowers, water, orange juice, honey and salt to the boil slowly
3. Remove from the heat and stir in the gelatin until it dissolves completely
4. Leave to stand for 10 minutes
5. Cover and refrigerate until it starts to solidify
6. Whip the cream until it stiffens
7. Fold the cream into the clover mixture
8. Place into individual serving bowls and refrigerate until set

White Clover Flour

This is an interesting type of flour that is made from white clover flowers. Pick flowers from an area not frequented by pets or sprayed with weedkiller. Just pick the flower heads without the stems. Rinse and dehydrate the flowers either using an oven on a low setting or a dehydrator.

Grind the dried flowers using a coffee bean grinder, blender or other device.

This flour has a nice 'green' smell to it that is reminiscent of peas, though anything you make with this flour will turn green. It is better used in savory dishes rather than sweet dishes.

Clover and White Chocolate Cookies

These cookies are made with a mixture of normal flour and white clover flour and are very tasty.

Ingredients:
- 1¼ cups brown sugar
- 1 cup butter
- 1 cup rolled oaks (uncooked)
- 1 cup all-purpose (plain) flour
- 1 cup white clover flour
- ½ cup white (granulated) sugar
- 12oz white chocolate chips
- 1 egg
- 1 egg yolk
- 1 teaspoon vanilla extract
- ½ teaspoon salt
- ½ teaspoon baking soda
- ¼ teaspoon ground cinnamon

Method:
1. Preheat your oven to 325F/160C
2. Cream the butter and sugar together

3. When smooth, add the vanilla extract, egg yolk and egg, stirring well
4. In a separate bowl, mix all of the dry ingredients together except the chocolate chips
5. Pour the wet ingredients into the dry and stir well until thoroughly combined
6. Fold in the chocolate chips
7. Divide into 24 dough balls (use a tablespoon)
8. Bake for 12-14 minutes, cool on a wire rack and serve

Clover leaves

Medicinal Uses

Clover is packed full of vitamins including A, B1, B2, B3, C and E as well as a whole host of minerals such as calcium, manganese, potassium, selenium and many more. It is a good source of fat and protein and contains fiber.

Also, red clover is a very good source of isoflavones which are a source of phytoestrogens which act like estrogen in your body. Research by the National Cancer Institute has shown that two of these phytoestrogens, daidzein and genistein, helps to hinder the growth of tumors. Because clover contains high levels of these phytoestrogens, it is not recommended for use by pregnant or nursing mothers.

In Chinese medicine, clover is used to make a tonic for

colds and to purify the blood. The Native American tribes used it to make a salve to treat burns. Traditionally, clover has been used for a wide range of respiratory problems including whooping cough. It is also used to treat skin conditions such as eczema and psoriasis.

Folklore, Myths and Legends

The origins of the stories surrounding four leaf clover are cloudy and very much depends on your religion. Christians believe that Eve took it from the Garden of Eden when she was banished to remind her of paradise. Others belief the four leaf clover is lucky because of the Druids, who collected them for their rituals.

Another thought is that it is considered lucky because it has four leaves. Four is an important number with four seasons, four elements, four cardinal directions, four evangelists in Christianity, four gates on the way to enlightenment in Sufism, and many more. Yet if you travel to some of the East Asian cultures, the number four is considered unlucky because it sounds very similar to the word for death. Some buildings in Asia actually skip the fourth floor because of this superstition.

The Celtic areas of Britain have a rhyme associated with the four leaves of the clover:

"One leaf is for fame,
And one leaf is for wealth
And one for a faithful lover,
And one to bring you glorious health
Are all in the four leaved clover."

The four leaf clover has many positive associations. It can help the bearer see the tricks of witches and fairies or help bring luck in love and protect them from evil. In the 17th century, clover was scattered in front of the bride to bring protection and luck in her marriage. It is thought that wearing a four leaf clover on your lapel will prevent you from being drafted by the military.

In modern times, the four leaf clover is remembered purely as a symbol of luck and of St. Patrick's Day. It is, however, found in a stylized form called a 'quatrefoil' which originated in Islamic art but became popular during the Renaissance in Gothic architecture. It is often found in churches and other religious establishments.

It is sad that in these modern times, we have forgotten the magic of the four leaf clover and explain it away as a genetic mutation. Even so, there is still something magical about finding one.

COLTSFOOT

Coltsfoot, *Tussilago farfara*, is a perennial plant that looks very similar to dandelions. Flowering in spring, this plant is unusual because the flowers have died back before the leaves start to appear. This is the source of its other name, "son before the father".

Before matches, the covering of this plant, which feels like felt, was dried, wrapped in a rag and dipped in saltpetre to make tinder.

The bright yellow flowers appear early in spring, before the leaves, which helps to distinguish it from dandelions and other similar flowers. The top of the leaf is smooth and looks waxy, while the underside has woolly, white hairs. In Southern Ontario, you can see coltsfoot flowering in April as the flower heads push through the remnants of the snow.

The flowers are about ½"/1.5cm wide and are bright

yellow. It is one of the first flowers of spring. The leaves are heart shaped and it grows to between 4-6"/10-15cm tall.

Coltsfoot will grow almost anywhere, often seen in ditches or roadsides. It likes a wet, poorly drained soil and is common in areas that flood in spring.

Gardening Uses

The leaves contain very high levels of calcium, magnesium and sodium, making it a good addition to the compost heap to add these minerals. Coltsfoot does not tend to grow in worked land, but instead prefers disturbed ground such as wasteland or arable fields.

Culinary Uses

The flowers can be used raw in salads where they add a pleasant aroma to the dish. They are used to sweeten other, bitter herbal teas. The dried flowers are chopped and used in pancakes and fritters. The young leaves are excellent in soups or stews, though can be used in small quantities raw in salads. Beer, known as cleats, and wine, referred to as clayt wine, can be made from this plant.

When cooked, the leaves are a little bitter, but washing the boiled leaves removes this bitterness. The dried and burnt leaves can be used instead of salt.

Coltsfoot Sorbet

This is an interesting use of coltsfoot to make a delicious sorbet.

Ingredients:

- 65 coltsfoot flowers (fresh)
- 3⅓ cups water
- 1 cup cane sugar
- 1 teaspoon fresh lemon juice
- 1 egg white

Method:

1. Remove the petals from the flowers by rubbing the flowers between your fingers into a bowl, ensuring none of the green sepals fall in
2. Put the water, sugar and petals into a pan and bring to the boil
3. Boil for 2 minutes, then remove from the heat and leave to cool for 20 minutes
4. Filter through a sieve and refrigerate the liquid until it is cold
5. Add the egg white and whisk well
6. Next, place the mixture into your ice cream maker or into the freezer
7. If using the freezer, whisk the mixture every 5 minutes for the first hour and then every 15 minutes until it has set

Medicinal Uses

Coltsfoot has anti-inflammatory and antitussive (treats/prevents coughs) properties. The root contains pyrrolizidine alkaloids and is potentially toxic, so not used. Small quantities of these toxins are thought to be in the leaves, but not at a concentration that is harmful unless an excessive amount of leaves are consumed. Boiling destroys these toxins.

Coltsfoot contains a substance called mucilage which coats the throat, providing a soothing effect. This herb is used to treat many ailments including laryngitis, wheezing, sore throats, bronchitis and asthma. In previous centuries, coltsfoot was smoked to help treat throat problems, but in reality this is unlikely to help the throat to heal.

Other uses for coltsfoot include as a topical balm on the skin, or using a poultice of flowers to treat stings, eczema and inflammation.

This herb is not recommended for children or pregnant women. It should not be used if you suffer from high blood pressure, heart disease or liver disease. When using as a tea, do not exceed 10g of coltsfoot.

Folklore, Myths and Legends

This plant is known as "son before the father" because the flowers often appear before the leaves. The name coltsfoot comes from the shape of the leaf which resembles the hoof-print of a colt.

In the 18th century, coltsfoot was a very popular herb and its image was used as the symbol of the apothecary trade. Coltsfoot has always been used as a smoking herb. Cornish tin miners used to smoke coltsfoot to stop them getting lung disease from their mining activities. Many respected herbalists such as Pliny and Dioscorides recommended smoking coltsfoot for its medicinal properties, but it was also burned in magical rituals to call out to a deceased loved one or to create balance. In the Americas, when coltsfoot was brought to the country, a blanket would be soaked in coltsfoot and then wrapped around someone with whooping cough to help treat and soothe it.

In Northern England, coltsfoot leaves were used to tell the future. The soft grey tissue of a new leaf was peeled away to leave a shiny surface which could be used as a mirror or window into the spirit world. When the right charm was spoken, the window showed you your future or the person you would marry. The chants were kept secret by the locals and have since been lost to memory.

COMFREY

Comfrey has a long association with humans and is not often cultivated at home as it is invasive and easily found in the wild. This herbaceous perennial, also known as 'knitbone', 'blackwort' or 'boneset' has large, lance-shaped leaves that are hairy. It grows with a central stem up to 3-4 feet tall. The bell-shaped flowers are blue or pink and even yellow. The root is black on the outside, white on the inside and grows very long and deep. Comfrey will grow back from any piece of root, making it extremely difficult to get rid of once established.

There are three main varieties found in the wild. There are cultivated varieties such as Bocking-14 which are non-invasive and can be bought for your garden. Non-invasive varieties are preferred by the gardener as they do not spread and take over.

- *Symphytum officinale* – wild or common comfrey
- *Sympthytum asperum Lepechin* – rough or prickly comfrey that is not safe to use internally
- *Sympthytum peregrinum* Lebed – Quaker, Russian or blue comfrey, a hybrid of rough comfrey that is also not to be used internally

Comfrey is loved by bees and can commonly be found growing by the side of streams and rivers in the wild. If you have an unused corner or your garden, then it can be worth planting comfrey there to use the leaves as fertilizer and to attract insects.

Gardening Uses

Comfrey has very deep roots, making it extremely difficult to remove once established. It pulls up nutrients from deep in the soil and stores them in their leaves, which are low in fiber and break down rapidly. Comfrey is an excellent plant to add to your compost pile and the leaves can be placed in trenches that other plants are grown in. The plant will grow even when covered in black plastic weed membrane.

Comfrey leaves are good on the compost pile, but add firmer plant matter to prevent the compost from becoming too gooey. The leaves can be rotted in water for a few weeks to produce a highly nutritious liquid fertilizer often referred to as 'comfrey tea'. This is an extremely good liquid feed when diluted for your plants.

Culinary Uses

While wild comfrey has been used as a food in the past, recent research indicates that comfrey can cause liver damage when taken internally and contains carcinogenic compounds. Russian and prickly comfrey have higher levels of these toxic alkaloids than wild comfrey, with the roots containing higher concentrations than the leaves. It is not recommended that comfrey is eaten.

The leaves do contain protein and some vitamin B12, which is rare in plants. Although the mature leaves are unpleasant to eat, the young leaves used to be eaten like a leafy vegetable.

Comfrey roots were dried and mixed with dandelion and chicory roots to make a coffee substitute.

Medicinal Uses
Wild comfrey has been a part of the herbalist's medicine chest for centuries. It contains allantoin, which is found in the milk of nursing mothers and encourages cell-reproduction and the healing of wounds. It also has a high mucilage content, which smooths skin. Comfrey works well when added to salves, lotions or even baths.

Comfrey is good as a poultice for breaks and strains and to reduce swelling. It is good in a salve for everything from abrasions to bruises to acne and burns.

However, comfrey should not be used for deep or puncture wounds because it can make the surface of the wound heal faster than the deeper parts, which results in abscesses. Before applying comfrey to any wound, clean it thoroughly so dirt is not sealed inside the wound.

When the roots are boiled, they produce a sticky paste that dries hard. This has been used to set bones, like a plaster cast, hence comfrey being known as 'bone-knit'. This paste is spread on a bandage which is then wrapped around the wounded area.

Wild comfrey can be used as a tea which will help speed the healing of broken bones and internal injuries. The root can be used as a tea to treat persistent coughs and ulcers.

While comfrey can cause liver damage and has carcinogenic compounds, they are at levels similar to those found in commercial medicines such as acetaminophen. If you keep your consumption of comfrey to a minimum and avoid prickly and Russian comfrey, then it is okay. It is recommended that pregnant or lactating women should avoid using comfrey in any form. Experts recommend using comfrey for no more than four consecutive weeks.

Folklore, Myths and Legends
Comfrey has been grown for healing since around 400BCE where it was used by Greek physicians such as Galen, Herodotus and Dioscorides. It has been used since this time and spread across Europe.

Comfrey is used magically to protect travellers and to prevent theft. Folklore says to put a comfrey leaf in your luggage to prevent it from being stolen or lost. Sachets of comfrey are placed in cars to protect them from being stolen. If you wrap money in a comfrey leaf before going gambling, it is believed to help your money to come back to you.

COMMON PLANTAIN

Common, or broadleaf, plantain, *Plantago major*, is a perennial weed that grows most of the year across Europe, Asia and North America, perhaps only disappearing in cold winters. It is also known as "rat's tail" plantain.

While we dig this up as gardener's, plantain is packed full of nutrients and very good for your health. It is used to treat chronic diarrhea and digestive tract disorders. As well as this, if you chew the fresh leaves a little, they can then be applied to the skin to treat open wounds, minor burns or insect bites! Typically, plantain is found growing in meadows, wasteland, gardens, roadsides and, most annoyingly, in your lawn. There are over 200 different species of plantain growing across the world. Common plantain can set seed in as little as six weeks and a single plant can produce over 14,000 seeds in a year so it can be very invasive.

Plantain grows in a rosette with oval shaped leaves with

thick stems, meeting at the base. When the stems are broken, you will see string-like veins that are similar to those found in celery. From the base, long shoots will come up that contain the small, pointed, green flowers that turn brown, and contains the seeds. The flower stalks can grow up to 1½ feet/45cm tall.

A relative of common plantain, ribwort (*Plantago lanceolate*) can often be found growing in similar conditions. The look very similar to each other, but ribwort has lance shaped leaves growing up to 10"/25cm long compared to the more oval leaves of rat's tail plantain. Both plantains are edible and have medicinal uses.

Gardening Uses

Plantain has no real use in the garden, though you can compost it. Avoid composting the seed heads unless you run a hot compost bin.

Culinary Uses

The whole plant is edible. The young leaves are eaten raw or cooked, though have a bitter taste our modern palette isn't used to. They are also quite time consuming to prepare as they taste better with the fibrous strands removed. Blanching the leaves in boiling water will make them more tender. The blanched leaves can be frozen and used in soups and stews.

The flower heads can be eaten raw or cooked. They need to be harvested before they turn brown and set seed. Interestingly, the seed heads taste very much like mushrooms.

Once a flower has gone to seed, it can still be used. It can be ground into a meal and used with flour in any recipe. The dried leaves also make an excellent, health-boosting herbal tea.

Baked Plantain

This is a simple recipe for plantain chips that can be eaten instead of potato chips and gives you a lot of healthy nutrients. This recipe takes about 20 minutes to make.

Ingredients:
- Extra-virgin olive oil
- Fresh broadleaf plantain leaves (washed and dried)
- Spices to flavor (as required)

Method:
1. Preheat your oven to 400F/205C
2. Put the leaves in a bowl, add a little oil and then season to taste
3. Line a baking sheet with parchment paper
4. Put the plantain leaves individually on the baking

sheet, ensuring they are not covering each other

5. Bake for between 3-10 minutes, depending on the size of the leaves (keep an eye on them as they can burn)
6. Serve immediately or eat later when cooled

Weed Soup

This is a lovely soup made from weeds in your garden! Best of all, the plants used in this are all nutrient dense and really good for you! Feel free to bulk out the soup with some root vegetables, but it is nice just the way it is. This recipe takes about 35 minutes to make and will serve 8-10 people. Add some extra bouillon cubes to give this more taste if you prefer.

Ingredients:
- 6 cups of chopped wild greens (e.g. plantain, dandelion, lamb's quarters, etc.)
- 7 pints/4 liters of vegetable broth
- 4 onions (finely chopped and sautéed)
- Spices to taste (e.g. garlic, pepper, salt, turmeric, etc.)

Method:
1. Put the broth in a large pan and heat
2. Just before it boils, add the onions, greens and spices, stirring to ensure they are mixed in (thicken by adding more onions and wild greens)
3. Simmer for 15-20 minutes, then serve

Medicinal Uses

Both ribwort and greater plantain have a number of medicinal uses. They are commonly used to tackle catarrhal conditions where, instead of suppressing the symptoms, the herbs help the body deal with too much catarrh.

Across Europe, ribwort is used for allergic conditions,

including hay fever, where the mucous membranes are overly sensitive or dry. Both plantains can provide help with a number of respiratory ailments including sinusitis and bronchitis as well as middle ear complaints.

Plantain is a very soothing expectorant, helping to relax irritating coughs where the airways tighten. Ribwort tea is a very good tonic for these conditions.

In the Middle Ages, plantain was used to treat tuberculosis. The famous herbalist Nicolas Culpeper (1616-1654) wrote that plantains are "singularly good herbs for those that are troubled with consumption of the lungs, or coughs that come of heat". He also mentioned how plantain was used to treat wounds, both fresh or old.

The leaves contain a substance called aucubun which is an antibacterial agent and increases the ability of the kidneys to excrete uric acid. Plantain also contains silica which helps your lungs to heal and repair damaged tissue, plus the plant contains zinc which boosts your body's ability to heal itself and defend against disease.

The high mucilage content provides an effective expectorant action. Together with tannin, also found in plantain, it soothes the lining of your gut.

For treating wounds, plantain is incredibly useful because there is usually some near to you. Chew a few leaves and then apply it to the wound. It will quickly stop bleeding and help 'glue' together broken skin because of the mucilage and astringent tannins. Plantains also have a mild antiseptic action, which helps to prevent infection. Use this mixture on insect bites and stings. The chewing of the leaves gets the juices flowing so they can be effective in helping you.

Folklore, Myths and Legends

Plantain is known as "Soldier's Herb" because of its use as a wound dressing. It has been used since prehistoric times and is referenced in the writings of the Anglo-Saxons and Shakespeare. It is associated with protection and used to

55

be hung in the home for this purpose.

COUCH GRASS

Couch grass, *Elytrigia repens*, is the bane of many gardeners for its long, invasive roots that get all over your garden. Also known as dog grass, witch grass and quack grass, it's common name, 'couch' comes from the Anglo-Saxon term 'civice' which means vivacious.

While couch grass is very invasive, it also produces a chemical which slows down the growth of other plants. It is common across Europe, Asia and North America. It can be grow for a hay which is fed to livestock and the tubular root is sometimes eaten by people when there is no other available food.

This perennial plant can grow to up to 32"/80cm tall with thin leaves. It does flower producing green flowers in July. The roots cover a large area and are extremely difficult to remove from the ground as the plant will grow back from broken bits of root. The roots usually have yellow colored tips. If you have couch grass in your ground, rotavating or otherwise mechanically digging the soil will result in spreading the root everywhere and creating even more plants.

Because couch grass is so invasive, it is rarely cultivated at home.

Gardening Uses

Couch grass doesn't have any uses in the garden as it is an invasive plant that competes with your plants for resources. It is best not composted as it can easily grow back from pieces of root.

Culinary Uses

Couch grass roots have a sugary flavor that is reminiscent of liquorice. The roots can be roasted and ground to make a flour, which is then made into bread or used as a coffee substitute.

Medicinal Uses

In Roman times, couch grass was used to treat kidney stones and improve urine flow. In the Middle Ages, the roots were used as a purgative for people suffering with constipation.

Today, couch grass root is used by herbalists to treat problems with the kidneys, gallbladder, prostate and urinary tract such as urethritis and cystitis. They are also used to treat rheumatism and gout. It is mildly diuretic. It is believed that couch grass is very good at dissolving kidney stones. When treating urinary tract infections, couch grass is often paired with herbs such as yarrow.

A couch grass decoction taken over several weeks is good at reducing inflammation of the prostate. A hot, wet pack of couch grass seeds placed on the abdomen was used to treat peptic ulcers. Juice extracted from couch grass roots has traditionally been used to treat liver disorders and jaundice.

To treat rheumatoid arthritis, simmer 1oz of couch grass root in a pint of water to create an infusion and then drink a wine glass full. Alternatively, a decoction can be prepared by boiling 2-4oz of root in a quart of water until it has reduced to one pint.

Folklore, Myths and Legends
Couch grass has been used as a herbal remedy since the Ancient Greeks where is was traditional used as a diuretic.

CROW GARLIC

Crow garlic, *Allium vineale*, is also known as wild garlic. It is very similar to chives with long, hollow, cylindrical leaves. It can be quite difficult to spot growing in the wild because it grows amongst tall grass.

The leaves die back over winter and the flowering stems start to appear in late spring. The flower heads appear in June with a papery sheath which falls off to reveal purple bulbils and pink flowers. The bulbils that form the flower head can be sprouted like small bulbs. The roots are ovoid in shape, looking like a tiny onion.

Crow garlic is found in a variety of locations including

meadows, hedgerows, parks, roadsides and growing with cereal crops.

Gardening Uses

This plant has no specific uses in the garden. It is rarely cultivated as plants such as chives are grown for a better flavor, but this plant is useful when foraging.

Culinary Uses

Crow garlic is used in the kitchen like onions and the taste is a cross between chives, onion and garlic. Collect the leaves in late winter and early spring, when they have the most flavor, and use like chives. Outside of this time, the leaves are rougher and have a less pleasant taste.

The bulbils can be used as a seasoning, either fresh or air dried. They can also be sprouted to add an oniony flavor to salads. The small bulbs underground will taste like a garlicky onion.

Medicinal Uses

The plant has many medicinal uses. It is a blood purifier, a diuretic, expectorant, carminative, stimulant and anti-asthmatic. A tincture made of crow garlic is used are a remedy for croup in children and to prevent colic and worms. The raw root eases shortness of breath and reduces bloody pressure.

Like other members of the onion family, this plant is generally beneficial to your health.

Folklore, Myths and Legends

Farmers dislike this plant growing in their pasture fields as it spoils the taste of milk. The juice of crow garlic can be used as a moth repellent and the plant as a whole repels moles and insects. Rub the juice of the plant on your skin to repel biting insects.

DANDELION

Dandelion, *Taraxacum officinale*, is considered an annoying, invasive, perennial weed by many people, yet is probably one of the most useful plants growing in your garden!

This early season, yellow flowered weed is packed full of vitamins, minerals and antioxidants, all of which are incredibly beneficial to you. For example, a single measuring cup of dandelion greens, uncooked, contains on average, 112% of your daily recommended intake of vitamin A and 535% of the amount of vitamin K you should take every day. It is one of the best healing herbs and every single part of the plant, except the flower stalk, can be used in some way.

While gardener's curse dandelion for its long taproot, this difficult to remove root brings up nutrients from deeper in the soil to shallow rooting plants. It helps to break up a heavy soil and adds nitrogen back into the soil. Best of all, as it flowers early in the season, usually mid-late April, it is a vital early season food source for many pollinating insects, including bees. I don't like to encourage the dandelions to spread in the vegetable garden, but I certainly allow them to flower for the bees and then I dead head them.

The dandelion is very easy to recognize from its yellow flower with somewhere between 150 and 200 yellow ray florets spreading outwards from the middle. The green leaves are very easily identified and the white seed heads are easy to spot and fun for children who like to blow the seeds all over your garden.

The leaves are toothy, with deep notches, growing in a rosette from the central taproot. They can be anything from 2"/5cm and upwards in length and are a favorite food of guinea pigs and rabbits. The dandelion can grow up to 12"/30cm tall, though its height does vary according to its surroundings. In a lawn, it will stay low to the ground to prevent it being mown, but in the wild, it can grow much taller as the lawn mower risk is not around.

Dandelions will grow literally anywhere from fields to scrubland to woods. They are commonly found in lawns, much to the annoyance of home owners, and will easily find their way into pretty much any area. If you are not going to allow them to flower, then remove the plants when they are young, before the taproot develops. This is a remarkably persistent weed because it has the ability to grow back from piece of taproot. While you can plant the seeds, dividing the long taproot will also create new plants. What this does mean, though, is that when you are removing dandelions, you need to be very careful not to break the taproot and to remove all of it from your soil.

Gardening Uses

As dandelions have very long roots, they can help loosen packed soil and draw nutrients from deep in the soil to the surface. As an invasive weed which grows back from pieces of root, most gardeners prefer not to give dandelions an opportunity to establish themselves because they then become very difficult to remove.

Culinary Uses

Dandelion is very useful in the kitchen. The leaves, root and flower are all edible. Because dandelion is a low growing plant, you need to be careful where you harvest it from as it could be contaminated with pesticides or animal excrement.

The leaves can be eaten raw in a salad as a salad green or can be cooked like spinach. They can be blanched and frozen or dried and stored for use over the winter. As the leaves age, they are better cooked, but young leaves are perfect for eating raw.

The flowers are useful in recipes or can be juiced. The root can be roasted and used as a coffee substitute.

Both the root and the leaves can be dried and used in herbal tea concoctions.

Dandelion Fritter Recipe
This is a great recipe that uses freshly picked dandelion flowers. Feel free to use any spices you like with this to give a more interesting taste.

Ingredients:
- 4 cups freshly picked dandelion flowers (washed)
- 2 cups all-purpose (plain) flour
- 2 cups milk
- 2 eggs

Method:
1. Mix the flour, eggs and milk together until thoroughly combined
2. Warm some olive oil on a medium heat
3. Hold the flowers by their underneath and dip them into the batter until they are thoroughly covered
4. Place the battered flowers in the skillet, flower side down
5. Once browned, flip and brown the other side. Flip multiple times if necessary to ensure an even, light brown color on the batter
6. Remove from the oil and drain on paper towels
7. Drizzle with honey or maple syrup or roll them in

it

Baked Dandelions
These are a great alternative to potato chips and are really easy to make! It takes about 20 minutes to make a batch and are delicious. Try combining this with some plantain leaves for a more interesting mix.

Ingredients:
- Large, fresh dandelions leaves (washed and dried)
- Extra-virgin olive oil
- Spices (whichever you like)

Method:
1. Preheat your oven to 400F/200C
2. Put the dandelion leaves in a bowl
3. Drizzle with oil and spices/herbs of your choosing
4. Mix well until thoroughly combined
5. Line a baking sheet with parchment paper
6. Put the leaves onto the sheet individually
7. Bake for 3-10 minutes depending on the size – the larger the leaves, the longer they need to bake with smaller leaves only taking 3-4 minutes
8. Eat warm or cold

Medicinal Uses
It won't come as a surprise to find that the humble dandelion has a whole host of medicinal uses as well. It is a very versatile herb that has a long association with health and healing.

Dandelion leaves are high in antioxidants which work to prevent harm caused by free radicals, thereby reducing the visible signs of aging and slowing cellular degradation. Dandelions contain beta-carotene, which protects the cells from damage. The flowers also contain polyphenols which are another antioxidant.

Dandelions are helpful in reducing cholesterol due to the bioactive compounds they contain. A 2010 study looked at the effect of dandelion on rabbits, https://www.ncbi.nlm.nih.gov/pmc/articles/PMC2820990/, and found that both the leaves and the root reduced cholesterol levels. A further study performed on mice, https://www.ncbi.nlm.nih.gov/pubmed/23603008/, found that eating dandelions reduced total cholesterol levels as well as fat levels in the liver.

There is evidence, though further research is required to substantiate the claims, that dandelions can help to regulate blood sugar levels in people with type 2 diabetes, https://www.ncbi.nlm.nih.gov/pmc/articles/PMC5553762/.

The compounds contained in dandelions help to reduce inflammation in the body according to a 2014 study, https://www.ncbi.nlm.nih.gov/pubmed/24447978. The study was performed on cells, but show that the chemicals in dandelions reduced inflammation in these cells.

Dandelions are high in potassium, which has numerous health benefits, but most importantly can help reduce blood pressure in people with high blood pressure. Although the study, https://www.ncbi.nlm.nih.gov/pubmed/26039623, showed potassium was effective in reducing blood pressure, research hasn't specifically been carried out into dandelions.

Other research indicates that dandelion can help reduce fat absorption and improve carbohydrate metabolism, meaning they can be useful in aiding weight loss. Other limited research shows dandelions can slow the growth of some cancers, including colon, liver and pancreatic, though a great deal of research needs to be performed before it can be proven beneficial.

Dandelions have antiviral and antibacterial properties,

meaning they can help to boost the immune system and keep you healthy.

As a traditional remedy, dandelion has been used for digestion issues and constipation. This is backed up by scientific research on rodents, https://www.ncbi.nlm.nih.gov/pubmed/21453412, though further research is needed.

All in all, dandelion is a very helpful and healing herb that is well worth adding to your diet.

Folklore, Myths and Legends
There is a lot of folklore associated with dandelions, which is to be expected given how long humans have been using the plant.

One way to determine if your partner loves you is to blow the seeds off a dandelion clock, though don't do it over someone's vegetable garden as they will get upset! According to folklore, if you blow all the seeds off with one blow, you are loved with a passionate love. However, if some seeds are left behind, your partner has reservations about your relationships. If a lot of seeds are left, then you are loved very little or not at all.

Folklore also says that dandelions can be used to tell the time. When you blow the seeds, the number that is left indicates the hour. This is where the origin of the term 'dandelion clock' came from when referring to the seed head. Known as the 'rustic oracle', it was used to tell the time by whether or not the flower was open. The flower opens around 5am in the morning and close again at 8pm. They were so regular that shepherds used the dandelion to help tell the time before watches were more common place.

The dandelion can also be used as a barometer and is surprisingly reliable. Once the seed head has formed, if it is open, then the weather will be good, but if the seed head shuts, then the weather is going to be wet. If the day will be showery, then the seed head will remain shut all the time, only opening when the wet weather has passed.

Dandelions are considered a lucky, beneficial plant. Brides would weave dandelion into wedding bouquets in the past as a symbol of good luck. In dreams, dandelions represent happy unions. Many of the old beliefs surrounding dandelions involved it bringing good luck or answering questions, mainly through blowing the seeds. Folklore says that blowing a dandelion seed head while making a wish would help the wish to come true.

In 18th century England, children would hold a dandelion under their chin and the more golden the reflection on their skin, the kinder and sweeter they were. If holding a dandelion under a child's chin produced a golden glow, then it would indicate the child would grow up to be rich. In more modern times, this was replaced with the buttercup.

When drunk as a tea, dandelion is said to increase physic abilities. Leaving a cup of steaming dandelion root tea by the bedside will call spirits to you. Burying dandelion in the northwest corner of a home will bring good favor to the household.

In theology, dandelion was one of the bitter herbs of the Passover and symbolic of grief and the Passion of Christ.

In folklore healing, the sticky white sap from inside the flower stalk was used as a cure for corns and warts.

Elderberry

Elder, *Sambucus nigra*, the tree the elderberry grows on, is commonly found in the wild where it grows like a weed. It is spread by bird droppings and can be found growing just about anywhere, from gardens to roadsides to scrubland and even on disused buildings. In its first year, it can be crowded out by faster growing weeds, but once established, it is very difficult to get rid of.

Its botanical name is derived from the Greek word "sambuke" which means musical pipe. Elder branches can easily be hollowed out, so they are ideal for making pipes. This deciduous plant is found across North America and Northern Europe and is one of the easiest plants to identify.

Elder will tolerate a wide range of soil conditions, though it does not like drought. It does best in fertile, moist, well-drained soils, but will grow in poor soils and still thrive. They grow in both sun and shade, though berries may ripen slightly later in shaded spots.

There are a number of varieties of elder growing wild and as cultivated varieties. Many of the cultivated varieties can be found growing in the wild where they have been spread by birds.

- *Sambucus nigra Aurea* – also known as golden elder as it has golden-yellow leaves with purple-black berries
- *Sambucus nigra* 'Black Beauty' – has purple foliage, flowers with a lemon scent and dark purple fruits, growing up to 8 feet/2.4m tall
- *Sambucus nigra* 'Black Lace' – has pink flowers, dark purple leaves and dark purple fruit, growing up to 8 feet/2.4m tall
- *Sambucus nigra f. laciniata* – has fern like leaves and purple/black berries
- *Sambucus racemose Plumosa Aurea* – a golden elder with bright golden leaves, preferring light shade, growing up to 6 feet/1.8m tall
- *Sambucus racemose Tenuifolia* – a dwarf red elder that produces few flowers and red berries, growing up to 4 feet/1.2m tall

While elder is a weed, it is a cherished plant by many foragers. The berries make a very beneficial winter cordial, can be used in jams and jellies and make a pleasant red wine. The flowers can also be made into a delicately flavored cordial or a delicious wine or champagne. It is quite a versatile plant and very easily found in the wild.

Gardening Uses
Elder is not usually cultivated as it is invasive, rapid growing and considered a weed by many gardeners. It is easy to find in the wild to harvest for flowers and berries.

Culinary Uses

The berries and flowers are used in the kitchen. The leaves are not edible, nor are the stalks on which the berries grow. They are mainly used to make wine or cordial. Elderberries are often thrown into crumbles or fruit pies and need to be thoroughly cooked before eating and should not be eaten raw. The flowers are best left outside for a couple of hours before use to allow any bugs to move out.

Elderberry Cordial

This is a traditional winter cordial that is very high in vitamin C and is excellent for boosting the immune system during the winter months. This cordial will last for up to two years.

Ingredients:
- Elderberries
- White (granulated sugar)
- Whole cloves

Method:
1. Cut the elderberries from the tree using a sharp pair of scissors just above where the single stalk starts
2. Strip the elderberries from the stalks using a fork. Remove as many stalks as you can
3. Put the elderberries into a saucepan and cover

them with water
4. Simmer for 20 minutes
5. Strain this mixture through a muslin bag, squeezing to get all the juice
6. For every pint of juice, use 1lb of white (granulated) sugar and 12 cloves
7. Add the juice, cloves and sugar to a large pan and boil for 10 minutes
8. Leave to cool
9. Bottle into sterilized glass bottles that have a plastic seal in the cap with an equal number of cloves in each bottle.

Elderflower Cordial

Elderflower cordial is the taste of spring and is wonderful mixed with sparkling water, wine, champagne or prosecco. It has a very delicate flavor that works well when drizzled over a fruit salad, added to jellies or berries or served with gooseberries.

Elder usually flowers from mid-May to mid-June. Pick the flowers on a sunny day in the morning, choosing the freshest looking flower heads, which will be frothy with creamy colored flowers.

Ingredients:
- 5½lb/2.5kg white (granulated) sugar
- 2 lemons (unwaxed if possible)
- 20 elderflower heads with as much stalk as possible cut off
- 3oz/85g citric acid

Method:
1. Put the sugar into a large saucepan with 2¾ pints/1.5l water
2. Heat gently, without boiling and stirring occasionally until the sugar has dissolved
3. Cut the zest from the lemons (a potato peeler is

helpful here), then slice the lemon

4. Once the sugar has dissolved, bring the syrup to the boil and then turn the heat off
5. Wash the flower heads and gently shake to dry a little
6. Put the flower heads into the pan along with the citric acid, lemon slices and lemon zest
7. Stir well, cover and leave for 24 hours
8. Line a colander with a piece of muslin or a clean tea towel and place it over a large bowl
9. Ladle the syrup into the colander and leave to drip through
10. Discard the solids left in the towel
11. Fill sterilized bottles with the liquid and keep refrigerated where it will last for up to 6 weeks

Medicinal Uses

The leaves of the elder are used in ointments to treat bruising, chilblains and sore muscles. The leaves are only used externally and never internally due to them containing toxic cyanogenic glycosides.

The flowers are a definite sign of spring and are popular with foragers. They are high in flavonoids which have anti-inflammatory and anti-allergy affects. Elderflower dries up excess mucus and reduces inflammation in the sinuses, making it very good for spring colds. Making a tea from elderflower and nettle is a great help for anyone who suffers from hay fever.

The flowers bring down a fever. A face wash made from the flowers evens out skin tones and reduces redness.

The berries are high in anti-oxidants and flavonoids as well as vitamins A and C. They are an excellent anti-viral and immune system booster, making the cordial a perfect winter drink.

Folklore, Myths and Legends

Elder has been used for thousands of years and the early

Europeans believed that this tree was inhabited by the "Elder mo'er" or mother. The spirit of the tree was greatly respected and according to tradition, it should never be moved or dug up without permission. In the Middle Ages, superstition was strong about elder, which would bring luck, health and happiness, so the trees were not cut or burnt as this would release the goddess the tree contained who would take her good fortune with her. Interestingly, burning elder releases cyanogenic glycosides, so food cooked over elder would be poisonous to eat and the gasses given off from burning it are noxious.

According to Christian tradition, Jesus was crucified on a cross made from elder and Judas hung himself from an elder tree.

FAT HEN

Fat-hen, *Chenopodium album*, is a very common weed found in gardens, also known as goosefoot, white goosefoot, lamb's quarters, pigweed or wild spinach. It is cultivated in Northern India where it is known as bathua. It grows across Europe and has naturalized in most other parts of the world. It prefers soils that are rich in nitrogen and is common on wasteland. Growing up to 5 feet/150cm, this is a commonly found weed that is very easy to identify.

This weed is a prolific self-seeder, so if you do not want it taking over your garden, dig it out before it sets seed and throw it on your compost heap.

From Neolithic times until around the 16th century, fat-hen was eaten as a vegetable and was eventually replaced by cabbage and spinach. It is rich in vitamin C and the seeds can be ground into a flour. It is a good source of vitamins when fed to chickens.

The seeds of this plant are notoriously difficult to get rid of and can last up to 20 years in the soil! They are broken down through composting, but are often introduced into gardens in horse or cow manure. If the manure if not fully rotted, fat-hen seeds can survive and will germinate in your soil.

Gardening Uses

Fat-hen is rarely cultivated these days as it is commonly found growing as a weed. It is not commonly eaten in the Europe or America as spinach and cabbage are preferred and produce a greater yield. It can be composted, but remove any seeds first.

Culinary Uses

The leaves and the seeds of fat-hen are edible. The plant flowers throughout the year, so harvest it when you see it is ready. The younger leaves are tastier and easier to eat than older leaves, so harvest the plant when it is young.

The seeds are high in starch and can be ground and added to flour or added whole to salads. The seeds can also be sprouted and eaten as micro-greens.

The leaves and young stem tips can be eaten like spinach and the water in which fat-hen is cooked can be used as a stock. The young flowers when they are budding can be steamed and eaten like broccoli.

Fat hen is high in protein and vitamins A, B1, B2 and C. It is also rich in phosphorus, iron, calcium, and omega 3 fatty acids.

Fat-Hen Pesto
This is a very simple recipe for pesto made from this tasty weed. It can be used in exactly the same way as basil pesto.

Ingredients:
- 3½oz/100g fat-hen leaves
- 1¾oz/50g pine nuts
- ½ cup/100ml extra-virgin olive oil
- Salt and pepper to taste

Method:
1. Blend the fat-hen and pine nuts until coarsely chopped
2. Season to taste with salt and pepper
3. Drizzle in the olive oil until you get the consistency you like

Medicinal Uses
Fat-hen doesn't have a lot of medicinal uses. Old herbal guides occasionally mention this plant as being used to treat gout, scurvy and sores. It is also useful in treating toothache, rheumatism and inflammation.

Some herbalists believe that the seeds are toxic when eaten in excess due to high levels of saponin. This can have a negative effect on anyone suffering from rheumatism, liver disease, intestinal inflammation or arthritis. The greens contain oxalic acid which can irritate the mouth when eaten in excess or raw.

Folklore, Myths and Legends

There is no folklore associated with this herb as it was typically just eaten.

FIELD MILK THISTLE

Field milk thistle, *Sonchus arvensis*, is known by many different names including swine thistle, field sowthistle, corn sow thistle, dindle, guyweed and tree sow thistle. It is a member of the daisy family and considered an invasive weed that reduces yield in farmer's fields. It looks similar to dandelion with its yellow flower heads and is attracts a wide variety of insects, including the beneficial hoverflies.

This plant is native to Europe, but has become naturalized across Russia, Australia, New Zealand and North America. It is commonly found by the side of a road, in fields or growing on the shores of rivers or lakes.

Sowthistle can grow up to 5 feet/1.5m tall with fewer leaves nearer the top and golden yellow flower heads. Its tall growth distinguishes it from dandelions, even though it produces a flower that looks very similar. This is a perennial plant and can be found throughout the year in most areas, though is more commonly spotted in July to October.

Gardening Uses

This is a weed that can crop up in your flower or vegetable beds and prolifically self seeds. If you find this in your garden, it is best removed before it sets seed and spreads everywhere. It has no real uses in the cultivated garden apart from it attracts hoverflies, so it is a good idea to allow this plant to flower before deadheading it. The plant can be composted, but do not compost the seed heads as they may not fully decompose before you use the compost.

Culinary Uses

The leaves, root and stem are all edible. The young leaves can be eaten raw or cooked like spinach. They have a slightly bitter taste, but work well in a salad with some sweeter greens. The leaves are high in vitamin C.

The stems can be cooked like rhubarb or asparagus, though sometimes there can be some prickles which are best removed but can be left on the stem.

The root is roasted and used as a coffee substitute.

Medicinal Uses

The leaves of the field milk thistle are used as a poultice as they have anti-inflammatory properties. A tea made from the leaves has been traditionally used to calm the nerves whereas a tea from the roots was used to treat chest complaints including coughs and asthma.

Folklore, Myths and Legends

This plant is believed to have got its name 'sow thistle' from the latex-like milk the stems exude when cut, which was thought to help mothering sows lactate.

The Latin name, "*Sonchus*" comes from Roman times and means "hollow", referring to the hollow steams of this plant. The "*Arvensis*" part of the name refers to the plant preferring to grow in cultivated areas.

Many of the common names of the plant refer to hares as sow thistle was considered a favorite plant of rabbits. Folklore says that a rabbit sitting beneath this plant cannot be disturbed by predators.

FIELD PENNYCRESS

Field pennycress, *Thlaspi arvense*, is a member of the brassica family growing up to 24"/60cm tall and flowering between May and July with spikes of small, white flowers. It is known by a variety of names, including stinkweed as it has a strong smell when crushed, as well as fanweed and mithridate mustard. This weed is native to Eurasia and North America. As the seeds are very high in oil, it is being investigated as a potential biofuel.

This weed is found on both cultivated land and on wasteland. Commercially, it is often grown in corn fields on rotation as it encourages more ground beetles. It is an adaptable plant, growing in both dry and moist ground, but prefers a nutrient rich soil. The seeds are quite persistent and after 10 years in the soil, have an 87% germination rate with some seeds even being viable after

30 years!

Gardening Uses

Field pennycress is not typically grown in the garden. It grows well in soils containing high levels of metal such as arsenic, lead and nickel and, over time, will decrease the levels of these metallic minerals. The plant can be composted

Culinary Uses

The young leaves are eaten raw or cooked, though harvest them before the plant flowers otherwise they have a very bitter taste. However, even the young leaves have a bitter flavor that not everyone will enjoy. They are best used in small quantities or cooked in soups or stews where they have a mustard/onion taste.

The seeds can be sprouted and used in salads or ground into a powder and used like mustard.

Medicinal Uses

Both the seeds and young shoots are considered to be beneficial for the eyes. The seeds are considered anti-inflammatory and act as a febrifuge. The whole plant has a strong antibiotic effect and is good for treating Staphylococci and Streptococci. The seeds are used in a herbal plaster, like mustard seeds, to ease muscle pain.

This is how you make a pennycress field plaster:

Ingredients:
- 8 tablespoons wheat flower
- 4 tablespoons pennycress seeds (ground)
- Pinch of ground ginger
- Pinch of ground cayenne pepper

Method:
1. Mix the wheat flower and pennycress seeds together and add some hot water to make the mixture into a paste
2. Add the cayenne pepper and ginger, stirring well and being careful not to get any near your eyes
3. To use, place a warm, damp cloth on the skin and then apply the paste on top of the cloth. Avoid applying the paste directly to the skin as it can cause irritation

Folklore, Myths and Legends

There is no known folklore associated with this plant.

Jason Johns

GROUND ELDER

Ground elder, *Aegopodium podagraria*, is known by a wide variety of common names including herb Gerard, bishop's goutweed, gout work, English masterwort and snow-in-the-mountain. It is a perennial plant in the carrot family, preferring to grow in shady locations. It name comes from the fact its leaves are similar to that of elder (described earlier in this book).

It is native to Europe and Asia but has been introduced across most of the rest of the world as an ornamental plant and is now considered an invasive plant in some areas due to the speed it spreads.

This plant can grow up to 3 feet/1 meter tall and does bear some resemblance to other plants, some of which are toxic with white umbrella shaped flower heads. The delicate white flowers are very popular with insects and will attract many beneficial insects to your garden, though it seeds prolifically and can quickly take over an area.

In its native area, ground elder is used as food for the caterpillars of several species of butterfly.

Gardening Uses

Ground elder works well in a wild garden or meadow where it will attract plenty of beneficial insects. It will take over, so some steps must be taken to control it and stop it crowding out other plants. It can be difficult to eradicate because it will grow back from any root fragments left in the soil. Removing the seed heads once the plant has flowered can help control the spread.

Weed killers are not very effective against ground elder and the best solution is to dig it out and then remain vigilant for a couple of years. It often makes its way into a garden through a piece of root in compost or manure.

Culinary Uses

The leaves were used up to the Middle Ages as a spring leaf vegetable and cooked in a similar manner to cabbage, though most commonly used in soup. The leaves should not be harvested after the plant flowers (around May/June in its native habitat) as the leaves have a pungent taste and act as a laxative. Pinching out the flower heads will stop the plant from flowering and the leaves can still be used in soups.

The leaves have an unusual, tangy flavor which isn't very popular with the modern palate.

Medicinal Uses

As a medicinal herb, ground elder was used to treat gout and arthritis, hence some of its names. In the past, the clergy, and particularly bishops, ate very rich food which caused gout, so they used this weed to treat it.

Boil the leaves and roots and then apply them as a hot wrap externally to the area to be treated.

The leaves, when eaten, have a diuretic effect and act as a mild sedative.

Folklore, Myths and Legends

The Romans are believed to have introduced the plant into Great Britain as a food plant. Monks took the plant to Northern Europe as a medicinal herb where it can still be found growing on monastic lands.

HIMALAYAN BALSAM

 Himalayan balsam, *Impatiens glandulifera*, is native to the Himalayas but has been introduced into the United Kingdom, Europe and North America, including Canada, as an ornamental plant where it has escaped into the wild. It was first introduced into England in 1839 where it was cultivated as an annual by gardeners as an alternative to orchids. In the USA, it is found in the more northern states as it seems to struggle in the hotter, damper southern areas. This plant has many different names from Policeman's Helmet to Gnome's Hatstand and even Kiss-me-on-the-mountain.

It is considered a very invasive plant, commonly found around waterways and on wasteland. Many local areas are spending a lot of money trying to eradicate this plant as it crowds out native plants and is not considered very useful for native insects either. As it produces a lot of pollen over a long period of time, many native pollinators focus on this plant and not on native plants. Removal is difficult as it is produces a lot of seeds and spreads them over a wide area.

This plant typically grows up to 6'6"/2m tall and has a stem with a red tinge or a soft green color. Some research indicates Himalayan balsam is an allelopathic plant, meaning it releases toxins into the ground to prevent other plants from growing and so increasing its competitive advantage. It flowers from July through to October, producing large, pink, bonnet shaped flowers and then green seed pods.

Gardening Uses
This is not a plant to cultivate in your garden, but one that can be foraged. When foraging for this plant, remove as many plants as you can by the roots to try and reduce the spread of it. As this is an invasive plant, it is an offence in many countries to plant Himalayan balsam.

The best way to control this plant is to uproot it and destroy it before it produces seed. Glyphosate does kill this plant as do other weed killers, but not everyone likes to use chemicals in their garden.

Culinary Uses
The green seed pods, seeds, young shoots and leaves are

edible. The flowers can be made into a parfait or jam. Himalayan balsam is eaten where it grows natively, particularly the seeds which have a nutty flavor. The seeds work very well in any curry dish. An oil can be extracted from the seeds which is used in cooking or in lamps.

The seed heads are explosive and throw seeds up to 22 feet/7m with each plant producing up to 800 seeds. The seeds remain viable for around two years and are often transported further by water. The seeds can be used in breads, cakes and biscuits. If you are harvesting the seeds, cover the seed heads with a paper bag before picking to prevent them from spreading. Again, once you have harvested the seed heads, uproot the plant to help reduce the spread.

The leaves, flowers, seedlings and young shoots are all edible raw or cooked, but should be consumed with caution as they contain a lot of minerals. Himalayan balsam also contains calcium oxalate which is harmful, but breaks down through cooking. Anyone with gout, arthritis, rheumatism, or kidney or bladder stones should avoid this plant as it can aggravate the condition.

Himalayan Balsam Syrup
This is a great recipe using the flowers which can be served

on desserts or pancakes. It can be cooked for longer to thicken so it is more like a jelly.

Ingredients:
- ½ cup/100ml water
- 9oz/250g white (granulated) sugar
- 1¾oz/50g Himalayan balsam petals
- Juice of 1 lemon

Method:
1. Gently heat the water and lemon juice
2. Add the sugar and stir occasionally until dissolved
3. Add the petals and the mixture should turn pink after about 5 minutes
4. Cook on a low heat, stirring regularly, until it reaches your desired consistency
5. Strain the mixture through a fine sieve and serve

Medicinal Uses

A homeopathic extract is made from Himalayan balsam and used to treat anxiety.

Folklore, Myths and Legends

There is no folklore associated with this plant.

JEWELWEED

Jewelweed, *Impatiens capensis*, is an annual native to North America, though the Pacific Northwest considers it invasive. It is typically found in ditches and near creeks. It has since been transported to Europe where it has naturalized. In America, it is favored by hummingbirds, but bees and butterflies also visit this plant.

This herbaceous plant grows up to 5 feet/1.5 meters tall and flowers from late spring to early fall. The flowers are usually orange, but can be blood orange or very occasionally yellow.

Gardening Uses

This plant is not typically grown in the garden due to its invasive nature.

Culinary Uses

Note that the berries are toxic to humans, particularly children and should be avoided.

The stems are cut up and cooked like green beans when they are young and tender. The young leaves and shoots can be cooked, though be aware this plant contains calcium oxalate crystals which can be toxic when consumed in large quantities, though it is usually destroyed in the cooking process.

Medicinal Uses

Jewelweed is not commonly used in modern herbal medicine and is considered dangerous when used internally. Therefore, this plant should only be used topically.

The juice of the stems and leaves of jewelweed is a traditional Native American treatment for skin rashes, including those from poison ivy and nettles. The fungicidal qualities of the stem juice have been verified scientifically and are an effective treatment for athlete's foot.

The sap is used to remove warts and a poultice made from the leaves treats cuts, burns and bruises.

Jewelweed Tincture

This tincture can be used externally to treat itching and skin rashes. It is applied using cotton balls or sprayed directly on to an injured area.

Ingredients:
- 1 quart jar
- Witch hazel (enough to fill the jar)
- Jewelweed stems, flowers and leaves (enough to tightly pack the jar)

Method:
1. Chop the jewelweed up and pack it into the jar
2. Cover with witch hazel and seal the jar
3. Put the jar in a crockpot and add water up to just below the neck of the jar
4. Heat the crockpot on low/warm and leave for 24-48 hours
5. Strain the tincture and store in brown glass bottles

Folklore, Myths and Legends
Also known as touch-me-not, jewelweed can often be found growing near poison ivy. If you touch the poison ivy, then you can break open the stems of the jewelweed and rub it directly on the affected area.

KUDZU

Kudzu, *Pueraria montana*, is a twining perennial vine that is a member of the pea family. In is native to east and southeast Asia and is considered invasive in the rest of the world, particularly North America. The plant is edible, but is frequently sprayed with chemicals to kill it, so check the plant carefully before harvesting.

Kudzu spreads mainly by runners and rhizomes. It rarely spreads by seed as each cluster of pods usually only contains a couple of viable seeds. It is an incredibly fast growing plant, easily growing 1 foot/30cm in a single day. In a single growing season, it can grow by as much as 60 feet/18 meters.

This plant is used to stop erosion and improve the soil. As it is a member of the legume family, it fixes nitrogen into the soil with its roots. It has deep taproots that bring nutrients up from deep in the soil to the surface layers. It is also grown as a livestock feed, being particularly useful in areas with poor soil.

The plant produces fibers which are used in making baskets. The long runners that propagate the plant and the larger climbing vines are great for weaving. The plant material is used green or split in half, dried and then rehydrated with hot water. The fibers are traditionally used to make clothing and paper and is used in the southern United States to make lotions, soaps and compost.

Gardening Uses
Due to the highly invasive nature of this plant, it is rarely used in the garden. For landowners, it may be planted to prevent soil erosion, but check local laws as it is illegal to plant in some areas.

Culinary Uses
Kudzu roots have traditionally been used as a food ingredient in Asia due to its starch content. In Vietnam, it is flavored with pomelo oil and made into a drink consumed in the summer. In Japan, the starch of the plant is known as kuzuko and it is used in a variety of dishes and as a substitute for cornstarch to thicken sauces.

The flowers can be used to make a jelly that is similar in

taste to grape jelly as well as syrups, candy and even home-made wine. The roots are high in iron, fiber and protein and are dried, then ground into a powder which can be used to coat fried foods or in a similar manner to cornstarch.

Kudzu Blossom Jelly
This unusual jelly (or jam in Europe) is great with cream cheese or melted slightly and served on ice cream and waffles. Note that the liquid from the flowers will be gray until lemon juice is added.

Ingredients:
- 4 cups Kudzu flowers
- 4 cups/1 liter boiling water
- 5 cups/1kg white (granulated) sugar
- 1 tablespoon lemon juice
- 1¾oz packet of powdered pectin

Method:
1. Wash the flowers in cold water and put into a large bowl
2. Pour the water over the flowers, leave to cool and refrigerate for 8 hours or overnight
3. The next morning, pour the liquid through a colander into a Dutch oven and discard the blossom
4. Add the lemon juice and pectin, then bring to a rolling boil, stirring constantly, over a high heat, for 1 minute
5. Remove from the heat and skim off any foam using a spoon
6. Pour the jelly into sterilized, hot jars, leaving ¼" headroom
7. Wipe the jar rims and seal
8. If desired, you can process the jars in a boiling water bath for 5 minutes to seal better

9.   Cool the jars on wire racks and then store

Kudzu Quiche
This quiche is made with kudzu leaves, though you can substitute any green such as spinach or kale.

Ingredients:
- 3 eggs (beaten)
- 1 9" unbaked savory pie shell
- 1 cup mozzarella cheese (grated)
- 1 cup young kudzu leaves and stems (chopped)
- 1 cup heavy (double) create
- ½ teaspoon salt
- Ground black pepper to taste

Method:
1.   Preheat your oven to 350F/175C
2.   Mix all the ingredients together in a bowl
3.   Pour into the pie shell
4.   Bake for 35-45 minutes until the middle has set

Kudzu Tea
This is a simple way to make tea from kudzu leaves.

Ingredients:
- 1 cup of kudzu leaves
- 1 quart water
- Sprig of mint
- Honey (to taste)

Method:
1.   Simmer the kudzu leaves in the water for 30 minutes
2.   Drain and serve with mint and honey

Medicinal Uses

Kudzu is used in traditional Chinese medicine where it is one of the 50 fundamental herbs, though little clinical research has been done on this plant. Kudzu can cause adverse effects if consumed by people who are taking tamoxifen, anti-diabetic medications, methotrexate or have hormone sensitive cancer.

Originating from East Asia, it makes sense that this plant has been used in traditional medicine for centuries. In Japan, kudzu powder is used in a herbal tea called kuzuyu. Traditional Chinese medicine use kudzu to make a herbal drink to treat a variety of symptoms including fever, stiff neck and headaches.

Folklore, Myths and Legends

Kudzu was introduced to the United States in 1876 at the World's Fair Centennial Exhibition in Philadelphia. The vine was not particularly popular with farms until 1935 when dust storms caused extensive damage to the prairies. Congress ordered kudzu to be used to prevent soil erosion and commissioned nurseries to grow over 70 million seedlings through the newly established Soil Conservation Service. Farmers, still sceptical about the plant but suffering from the effects of the dust storms, were offered as much as $8 an acre (around $150 in current terms) to plant kudzu to battle soil erosion.

The government went on a major offensive to persuade farmers to plant kudzu and hundreds of thousands of acres of the southern States were planted with this rapidly growing vine. This vine was planted by the sides of railroads and highways to cover the damage they did to the local environment.

By 1945, over a million acres were planted, though much of it was grazed by animals or plowed into the ground as farmers struggled to make any money from this plant. By the 1950's, the Soil Conservation Service was distancing itself from kudzu.

The vine left by roadsides and railroads, was unchecked

Jason Johns

by grazing and started to grow in its monstrous way, creating a series of myths about a vine that grows very rapidly. Many people in the southern States grew up fearing this vine because of its ability to grow quickly with the myth that snakes lived in its depth.

MALLOW

Common mallow, *Malva neglecta*, is a member of the *Malvaceae* family which includes okra, hibiscus and cotton. It is an edible plant and has medicinal uses as an anti-inflammatory, diuretic, laxative and more.

It has flexible stems from a central point, often creeping along the ground and produces round fruit with cheese like wedges, giving it the nickname of 'cheese plant'. It roots from both seeds and broken stems, creating a deep tap root. Its flowers have white, pink or lilac flowers with 5 petals. Mallow grows up to 2 feet/60cm long.

Common mallow can be found growing across Europe, Australia, Asia, the Americas and Northern Africa. Often found growing on waste land, by the side of the road or in your garden, it is a surprisingly common weed.

Gardening Uses

Mallow is likely to pop up in your garden as it does spread easily. Beyond composting, there is no specific gardening uses for this plant.

Culinary Uses

All parts of this plant can be eaten. The leaves and flowers can be eaten in salads and the fruit can be used like capers. The leaves, when cooked, create a mucus like okra does, so is good to thicken stews or soups. The leaves have a mild flavor and can be dried and used to make a tea. The leaves contain high levels of vitamins A and C and also iron, potassium, selenium, magnesium and calcium.

When the roots are boiled, they release a thick mucus that can be beaten to create a meringue substitute for egg whites.

Medicinal Uses

The Native Americans used mallow to heal sores and swellings through poultices and infusions. In Roman times, as recorded by Pliny the Elder (23-79AD), a decoction of the root was used to treat dandruff and the warmed juice of the plant helped with melancholy. The Romans boiled the leaves in milk to help cure coughs. A side effect of the plant was it had a mild laxative effect.

Ground mallow seeds are used in Pakistan to treat coughs and bladder ulcers whereas the Italians use mallow tea to reduce inflammation and as a gargle to ease sore throats.

Modern science has discovered that mallow as both anti-fungal and antimicrobial properties. An extract of mallow has been patented as an acne treatment. Extracts from the plant mixed with ethanol have been shown to have a promising effect treating Staphylococcus and the plant is currently being investigated as a treatment for hypertension.

Folklore, Myths and Legends
Pliny the Elder wrote that sprinkling mallow seeds onto your genitalia promotes sexual desire, i.e. acts as a sexual stimulant. The Iroquois tribe used mallow as a love medicine.

When Pythagoras (570-495 BCE) went for extended visits into shrines, he would prepare a meal with mallow leaves to prevent him from getting hungry and another using mallow seeds to prevent him feeling thirsty.

MARE'S TAIL / HORSETAIL

 Horse tail, *Equisetum arvense*, is a very common weed that is the bane of many a gardener because it is extremely hard to get rid of. Many people refer to this plant as mare's tail, but this is misapplied as mare's tail refers to a similar, aquatic plant. It does bear some resemblance to asparagus, which can cause some confusion.

In the spring, it sends up a brown stem that has spore cones on top. The spores are then released and the weed turns green. It has been around since the time of the dinosaurs (Carboniferous period) in one form or another, which gives you an idea of how difficult it is to kill! Back in the Carboniferous period, horsetail grew much taller and today we can still find fossils of its prehistoric relative which are known as Calamites.

It spreads via underground rhizomes and produces above ground shoots which can be up to 3 feet/1 meter tall. The roots can go down to 6 feet/2 meters or more. It grows pretty much anywhere and is a very invasive weed.

It is found in most places across the northern hemisphere. While it is found in the southern hemisphere, it is less common.

Horsetail can accumulate a variety of elements in its tissues, including zinc, lead, copper, cadmium and even gold! It contains high levels of silica, which makes the stems rough and abrasive. An extract of horsetail is a strong fungicide that is used to treat rust in mint and blackspot on roses. This plant contains so much silica that the stalks can be used as to polish metal or clean milk buckets. One of its common names, pewterwort, gives you an idea of its use.

Note that this plant is toxic to most livestock, particularly horses.

Gardening Uses
This plant has no use in the garden and you do not want to encourage into your garden in any way. It is an extremely invasive plant and virtually impossible to get rid of once established.

It often makes its way into gardens via manure and will spread from even a tiny piece of root. If you do find this in your garden, dig out as much of the root as you can every time you spot it. Be aware that the roots can go down some distance and are difficult to get out. Do not compost this plant as it can easily spread if it has not fully broken down. Burn or otherwise destroy this plant. Chemicals do not work very well against this plant, but some strong chemicals can work if injected into the plant.

Culinary Uses

Horsetail can be eaten in soups, stews or stir-fries or makes for a healing tea. In spring, the tan shoots containing spoors are edible. The later green shoots are typically used as medicine rather than eaten.

Pinch the young shoots off close to the ground and peel off the brown, paper like sheaf around the nodes. Finally, pull off the top cone and eat the tender stems between the nodes. These can be dipped in oil or cut up and added to soups or stews.

The green tops are harvested when the leaves are a vibrant green color and pointing up or out, typically between March and July. As the plant ages, the leaves droop and turn an army green color. In these older plants, the silica crystalizes in the leaves and is less water-soluble, meaning it is not so good for us to eat.

The green stalks contain thiaminase, which destroys thiamine (vitamin B1), so should not be eaten raw. Drying or cooking destroys this enzyme, making it safe to eat. Horses are particularly keen on horsetail, and it is not good for them.

When harvesting horsetail, avoid gathering it in areas which has water draining onto it from industry or agriculture. Horsetail absorbs inorganic nitrogen compounds to create toxic alkaloids.

Medicinal Uses

Horsetail has been used for centuries as a medicine. The Roman physician Galen, 129-199AD, used horsetail to treat a variety of ailments including kidney or bladder problems and arthritis. This plant is also known as an antibiotic, antiseptic, astringent, diuretic and anti-haemorrhagic.

The plant is one of the richest sources of silica in the plant kingdom, but also contains vitamins A, E and C as well as manganese, magnesium, calcium and potassium.

Horsetail tea is high in quercetin, which is an anti-inflammatory compound that is particularly effective against allergic reactions. When mixed with mullein leaf, it makes a tea that is very good for people who have asthma. Horsetail has been used to treat tuberculosis, bronchitis and urinary tract infections.

As horsetail is so high in silica, it is great for strengthening bones, skin, cartilage, hairs, nails and arteries. It is used to help treat hair loss and stimulate hair growth.

Horsetail tea is easy to make from a large handful of herb for 2-3 cups of water. Steep for anywhere from 15 minutes and drink 2-3 cups regularly for best effect. This plant combines well with other herbs such as nettle, peppermint and red clover to make a tea that is excellent for hair, bones and nails.

Horsetail is used in cosmetics as a skin tonic and a hair wash due to its high levels of silica. The tea can be applied to the skin to help recover from sunburn or to improve the quality of the skin.

A simple hair rinse can be made by boiling 6-8 cups of water, removing it from the heat and adding a cup of dried horsetail. Leave it to cool until warm and then strain. Pour the tea over your hair or, if you have long hair, allow the hair to sit in the bowl with the tea. If you catch the tea in another bowl and keep pouring it over your hair, you end up with silky and shiny hair.

Folklore, Myths and Legends
The folklore surrounding this plant relates to its medicinal uses.

MULLIEN

Mullein, *Verbascum thapsus*, is native to Asia, north Africa and Europe, but has been introduced to Australia and the Americas. It is a tall, hairy biennial, growing up to 7 feet/2 metres, producing a tall stem in its second year with a dense spike of yellow flowers. It spreads easily from seeds, but is not considered invasive.

Its common name, mullein, comes from German and means 'king's candle' due to its sceptre like growth. It is known by a variety of other names, including cowboy toilet paper (common in the western United States), beggar's blanket and more. In the 19th century, it was known by over 40 different common names just in the English language! Quite a few of its names derive from the fact that the thick, silvery leaves were used as toilet paper.

The tall flower is easily identifiable and can be up to two feet (60cm) long. The flowers are about ¾"/2cm across and have five petals, five hairy green sepals, a pistil and five stamens. Mullein flowers in the summer and they last for about six weeks. Only a few of the flowers are blooming at any time, with each flower being replaced by a seed capsule once the flowering has finished.

Mullein can be found growing in the wild in fields, waste ground and any dry, sunny area.

Gardening Uses
As this plant is a common weed and seeds profusely, it is not commonly grown in the garden. It may be composted, but remove any seed heads first.

Culinary Uses
Both the leaves and flowers are edible and can be used in salads, but are more commonly made into a tea. The tea is traditionally used to help stop coughs and ease an irritable bladder. Simply steep a couple of teaspoons of dried mullein in boiling water for 10-15 minutes and then strain as the hairs on the leaves can sometimes irritate the throat.

Commercially, mullein is used in some alcoholic drinks as a flavoring.

Medicinal Uses
Mullein has anti-inflammatory and anti-viral properties, making it a great plant to have during cold season. It has traditionally been used for lung complaints such as asthma, colds and coughs. It can be mixed with honey and elderberry to make a very effect cough syrup.

This herb also acts as a diuretic and has a mild sedative effect. It is used direct on the skin to treat bruises, skin infections, haemorrhoids, burns, wounds and even frostbite.

Folklore, Myths and Legends
Roman soldiers used to dip the plant stalks in grease to create torches and many other cultures used the leaves as wicks. American colonists and the Native Americans used mullein leaves to line their shoes to keep their feet warm.

According to tradition, mullein could ward off evil spirits and curses.

The seeds contain compounds that are toxic to fish and it is used to clear unwanted or invasive fish from ponds or waterways.

NETTLES

Stinging nettles, *Urtica dioica*, are a common sight in many a garden or hedgerow and most of us are well aware of its mildly painful sting. Originating in Asia and Europe, it has now spread across the globe. There are about 30-45 different plants in the nettle family, including the white flowered dead nettle, but this chapter is dedicated to the stinging nettle.

Humans and stinging nettles have a relationship that dates back thousands of years. Roman soldiers stationed in Britain used to beat their legs with nettles to keep themselves warm. The nettle is one of the first 'greens' to appear after the cold of winter and is full of vitamins so was treasured by ancient man. Chlorophyll is extracted commercially from nettles in Europe to make a green food coloring known as E140. It has a wide range of medicinal uses and when dried, makes an excellent livestock feed through winter.

Nettles are very easy to identify and most gardeners have picked one accidentally while weeding and experienced the pain of its sting. The pain of the sting is eased by rubbing the affected area with a crushed dock leaf. The skin will raise up where you have been stung and in some people it is more pronounced than others. The sting comes from formic acid which is contained at the base of each of the hollow hairs on the plant. Formic acid is commonly found in ant stings too.

Nettles will grow from 3-7 feet/1-2 meters tall and are found in hedgerows or on waste ground, often growing in areas abandoned by humans. It can indicate a fertile soil. Nettles are an important plant for the larvae of several butterfly species, including peacock butterflies and the small tortoiseshell. Some moths also use it as a food for their caterpillars and the ghost moth larva eat the roots. Although found in meadows, it prefers wetter ground where it will spread not only by seed, but also by rhizomes, making it extremely hard to eradicate.

Nettles can also be used to make fibers for clothing and to make paper.

Gardening Uses
Nettles are not often cultivated as they are a common weed. They are good to have in your garden in a 'wild' patch, but can spread very easily and are a valuable food

for wildlife. The nettles can be composted and make for a very good liquid compost when stewed in water for a few weeks.

Culinary Uses

This common plant was once a staple food for early man. After the cold of winter when early humans were often suffering from vitamin deficiency, this plant was a welcome source of nutrients.

All the leaves are edible, but the younger leaves are preferable. Until dried or cooked, nettles will have their stinging hairs, so never eat them raw. Nettles can be cooked and eaten like spinach or added to stews or soups. Beer can be made from the young shoots and the root is used medicinally.

Nettles are rich in vitamins A and C as well as calcium, iron, manganese and potassium. The leaves are best eaten young, before the plant flowers as the leaves develop cystoliths after flowering, which are gritty particles that can irritate the urinary tract. If you suffer from an iron deficiency, then nettle tea is an excellent drink that will help increase your iron levels and better for you than most supplements!

Cornish Yarg is a cheese made in Cornwall, England that uses nettles. It is quite unique and has a taste similar to Dutch Gouda. Nettles are used in a lot of dishes across the world, including Greek hortopita and Albanian borek.

Nettle and Leek Soup
This is a very tasty soup that is also good for you. It takes about an hour to make and this recipe will serve 4-6 people.

Ingredients:
- 2 large potatoes (cut into small chunks with the skin left on)
- 10 cups of water

- 4 cups leek (thinly sliced)
- ½ cup dried stinging nettle
- Handful of fresh dandelion leaves (finely chopped)
- Handful of fresh red clover flowers
- 3 teaspoons garlic powder
- 3 teaspoons dulce flakes (reserve one teaspoon for garnish)
- 2 teaspoons dried thyme
- 1 teaspoon salt
- 1 teaspoon ground pepper

Method:
1. Par-boil the potatoes, then drain and rinse
2. Put the water into a separate pot and add the stinging nettle
3. Bring to the boil, reduce the temperature and add the rest of the ingredients
4. Stir well, then simmer for half an hour
5. Blend the soup until smooth and serve, garnished with fresh parsley and/or dulce flakes

Nettle Pesto
This is an alternative to pesto made with nettles. Use it like you would basil pesto. This pesto is thinner than regular pesto and will store for 3-5 days in your refrigerator.

Ingredients:
- 1 cup olive oil
- ½ cup blanched nettles
- ¼ onion (chopped)
- 2 lemons (zest and the juice)
- 2 garlic cloves (crushed)
- ¼ teaspoon chilli flakes
- Salt and pepper to taste

Method:
1. Put the garlic, onion and nettles in a blender and drizzle in the olive oil as you blend until you reach the desire consistency
2. Add the lemon zest and juice, then blend until smooth
3. Add the chilli flakes and season to taste and blend once more.

Stinging Nettle Beer
This is a great beer to make and is full of nutrients. Just make sure the nettles are thoroughly cleaned first otherwise you may discover unwanted bugs in your beer. This recipe will make around 7 pints/4 liters. To make the beer more bitter, add a large dandelion root. To make a spicier beer, add a large ginger root.

Ingredients:
- 11lbs/5kg young nettle leaves
- 7 pints/4 litres water
- ½ cup boiled water (cooled to around 77F/25C)
- 1 cup brown sugar
- 3½oz/100g cream of tartar

- 1 sachet of wine yeast
- Juice of 2 lemons
- Juice of 2 oranges

Method:
1. Boil the nettle leaves, together with the ginger or dandelion root, in the water for 30 minutes
2. Strain off the nettles, squeezing out as much liquid as you can, keeping the liquid
3. Add the cream of tartar, brown sugar and orange/lemon juice to the liquid and stir well
4. Add to a fermenter with a lid and leave overnight to cool to 68-80F/20-27C
5. Sprinkle the yeast into the cooled boiled water and stir until it has sunk
6. Stir the yeast carefully and then pour evenly into the fermenter
7. Cover the fermenter and wait until the foam has collapsed, which will take 3-5 days keeping at a constant temperature of 68-80F/20-27C
8. Bottle and enjoy

Medicinal Uses

Nettles have a wide variety of medicinal uses and are currently being studying as treatment for a number of complaints.

A 2009 study gave people a supplement containing nettle to relieve pain from arthritis. (https://www.ncbi.nlm.nih.gov/pmc/articles/PMC3003499/). Over a three-month period, those who were taking the stinging nettles reported fewer symptoms and had less need to take anti-inflammatory medicine. An extract of nettle appears to have good pain relieving effects.

Stinging nettles are also effective in treating seasonal allergies, though more research is required to work out exactly how this works.

In a 2013 study, type 2 diabetics took 500mg of

stinging nettle extract every 8 hours and over three months, this had a positive effect on their blood sugar levels. Again, more studies are required, but the early results are positive.

Traditionally, nettle root has been used to treat an enlarged prostate and difficulty urinating. Make the root into a tea and drink throughout the day for the best effect.

Nettle tea, made from the young shoots is very rich in iron, helping coagulation and the formation of haemoglobin. This tea is very effective in treating iron deficiency as the iron in nettles is very easily absorbed by humans.

Folklore, Myths and Legends

Nettles have quite a lot of folklore associated with them. In the story, "The Wild Swans" by Hans Christian Andersen, a fairy instructs the heroine to gather nettles from the graveyard at night and spin the fibers into yarn to knit into coats for each swan brother to break the spell.

According to the Anglo-Saxon "Nine Herbs Charm", dating back to the 10th century, nettles were used to protect people from 'elf shot' which are mysterious pains in both humans and livestock caused by arrows shot by elves.

In Norse mythology, nettles are associated with Thor, the god of thunder, and Loki, the trickster god. Loki owns a magical fishing net made from nettles. According to the ancient Celt, thick groups of nettles indicates that fairies are living nearby.

Nettle oil was used before paraffin become common, the juice was used to curdle milk and seal leaky barrels. Tradition says that nettles drive frogs from beehives and flies from larders.

PURPLE DEADNETTLE

Purple deadnettle, *Lamium purpureum*, translates from Greek as "the devouring purple monster". It is an annual weed with easy to spot reddish/purple flowers and leaves. This nettle does not sting and is safe to pick, plus is a member of the mint family, noted by its square stem.

This plant flowers in April, and after about six weeks of blooming, produces seeds. The flowers are much loved by bees, particularly as they appear early in the season. The upper leaves have a red/purple tinge to them and, when dried, used in a poultice which stems bleeding.

Jason Johns

Purple deadnettle will grow up to 1 foot/30cm high, though is often a much shorter plant. It can be found growing on wasteland and on roadsides across Europe, western Asia, the Mediterranean and northern Africa. It has been introduced into North America where it is now a common sight in many areas.

Gardening Uses
Purple deadnettle is not typically grown in a garden. It is a good addition to any wildlife garden as it attracts insects. It is also good on the compost pile.

Culinary Uses

Purple deadnettles are easy to harvest, just cut the stems close to the ground and shake to get rid of bugs and dirt. The plant, like other members of the mint family, reproduce from the roots, so cutting the leaves doesn't stop the plant from growing or spreading. Only the leaves are edible, so discard the stems. The leaves work well in a salad or in smoothies.

This plant contains high levels of vitamins A and C, as well as iron. The leaves have a rich, earthy flavor and can be used in any recipe like you would use spinach. The leaves are great in soups, casseroles, salads and stir-fries. They can be dried for use later in the year in teas. Use three tablespoons of dried leaves for every cup of boiling water, steep for 5-8 minutes and then strain and sweeten to taste. Purple deadnettle blends well with a number of other herbs such as dandelion root, milk thistle and burdock which will support the function of your liver and kidney.

Deadnettle Pilaf
Purple deadnettle is easily foraged and makes a nice addition to this rice dish. It will take about 45 minutes to

make and serves 4-6 people.

Ingredients:
- 2 garlic cloves (minced)
- 1 large shallot (diced)
- 2 cups fresh purple dead nettle leaves (rinsed and patted dry)
- 2 cups chicken/vegetable broth
- 1 cup long-grain rice
- 2 tablespoon butter
- 1 teaspoon salt

Method:
1. Heat the butter in a medium sized saucepan that has a lid
2. Once it has melted, add the shallot and cook until softened, 4-6 minutes
3. Add the garlic and cook for a couple more minutes until fragrant
4. Add the rice and stir well so the grains are covered with butter
5. Stir in the dead nettle leaves and cook for another 3-5 minutes until wilted
6. Add the salt and mix well
7. Pour in the stock and bring to the boil
8. Reduce the heat to a simmer, cover and cook for a further 15 minutes
9. Remove from the heat and fluff the grains up with a fork before serving

Deadnettle Rice Bake
This is an interesting dish, easy to make and can be enhanced by adding any other vegetables you fancy.

Ingredients:
- 1 cup milk
- 1 cup cooked rice
- 1 cup deadnettle leaves (washed and dried)
- ¼ cup cheddar cheese (shredded)
- 1 garlic clove (minced)
- 1 small onion (chopped)
- 1 egg
- 1 tablespoon soy sauce
- 1 tablespoon extra-virgin olive oil
- 1 teaspoon salt
- 1 teaspoon pepper

Method:
1. Heat the oil in a heavy frying pan on a medium heat
2. Add the garlic, nettle leaves and onions and cook for 2-3 minutes
3. Put the rest of the ingredients into a mixing bowl and mix well
4. Add the onions and garlic to the mixing bowl and stir until well combined
5. Pour the mixture into an 8"x8" greased baking dish
6. Cook at 350F/175C for 30-35 minutes, then serve

Medicinal Uses
Purple deadnettle has a variety of medicinal uses and works as a diuretic, purgative and astringent as well as anti-bacterial and anti-fungal properties. The fresh leaves can be used as a poultice on cuts.

Folklore, Myths and Legends
In some areas, this plant is known as 'purple archangel' because it flowers around May 8th, which is the Feast of the Apparition, when archangel Michael appeared at

Mount Gargano in Italy in the 6th century.

PURSLANE

Purslane, *Portulaca olearacea*, is a succulent annual trailing plant that thrives in poor soil growing to about 4"/10cm high. It is found across north Africa, Europe, Asia, Australasia and the Middle East. It is not so common in the United States but is believed to have made its way there in pre-Columbian times by unknown methods where it was eaten by Native Americans.

This weed is very nutritious and has a reddish, thick stem and fleshy, succulent green leaves. The flowers are quite small and yellow in color with five petals, typically open for a few hours on bright sunny mornings. Purslane flowers from the middle of summer through to September or October, depending on the climate. The flowers turn into seed capsule, containing small, black seeds, which spread easily.

Purslane can be found in cracks in pavements or in

cultivated ground, waste ground, fields or by the side of the road. It's a fairly versatile plant and has no objections to growing in poor quality soil.

Gardening Uses

Purslane can be grown as a crop, though is not commonly sown. It grows very rapidly and carpets the ground densely, preventing sunlight getting to the soil and any seedlings below it. It can be helpful to keep weeds down on uncultivated soil and can be composted, though dispose of any seed heads separately.

As purslane covers the ground well, it can help to lock moisture into the ground and create a humid microclimate for other plants near to it. It has deep roots that bring up nutrients and moisture from deep down, plus it helps to break up hard soil.

Culinary Uses

The leaves, stems and flower buds are edible and can be eaten as a cooked vegetable or served in soups, stews or salads. It has a slightly sour and salty taste due to oxalic and malic acid.

The Aboriginal Australians make seedcakes from purslane seeds while the Greeks eat this plant in salads and in a dish with feta cheese, onion, garlic, olive oil, oregano and tomatoes. In Turkey, it is eaten as a baked vegetable, cooked like spinach, used in salads or used with yogurt to make something similar to tzatziki. The Egyptians also eat purslane, but only cook it rather than eat it raw.

The plant is quite nutritious, being high in vitamins E, C and A as well as containing Omega-3, magnesium, manganese and iron.

Fried Purslane
This is a very quick and easy dish to make. Rather than frying, it can be baked in the oven at 300F/150C for 15 minutes.

Ingredients:
- 1 cup purslane leaves and stems
- ½ cup all-purpose (plain) flour
- 1 egg (beaten)
- Panko bread crumbs

Method:
1. Mix the flour, egg and purslane together
2. Divide into small patties or leave as one large patty
3. Cover with the bread crumbs
4. Cook in butter or oil, turning occasionally, until golden brown all over

Purslane Egg Cups
This is a nice breakfast or snack that is very good for you. This recipe will make 12 egg cups and take about 40 minutes to make.

Ingredients:
- 2 cups purslane (chopped)
- 2 onions (finely chopped)
- 1 small bell pepper (chopped)
- ¼ cup shredded cheddar cheese (alternatively, substitute some crumbled feta for some cheddar)

- ¼ cup milk
- 12 eggs
- Salt and pepper to taste
- Any spices of your choosing

Method:
1. Preheat your oven to 350F/175C and grease a muffin pan
2. Cook the onions and peppers in butter or oil for 5-7 minutes until softened
3. Put the eggs, milk, cheese, onions, peppers and spices of your choosing in your food processor and blend well
4. Stir in the purslane
5. Divide evenly across the muffin tin
6. Bake for 20-25 minutes until the egg is fully cooked
7. Eat warm or cool and store in an airtight container in your refrigerator where it will last for 2-3 days

Medicinal Uses
Purslane is a useful medicinal plant, being a diuretic, febrifuge and having antibacterial properties. It is part of traditional Chinese medicine where it is used to treat diabetes and hypertension, though this has not been backed up by modern, scientific research.

This plant was known to the ancient Egyptians, Romans and is even mentioned in Greek medical texts dating to around 600BC. It was used to treat intestinal worms, dysentery, sore eyes and dermatitis.

Folklore, Myths and Legends
Purslane was believed to guard against evil spirits, but it needed to be scattered around the person's bed. According to Chinese folklore, purslane is a "vegetable for long life" and has long been a part of Chinese medicine.

Jason Johns

ROSEBAY WILLOWHERB

Rosebay willowherb, *Chamerion angustifolium*, also known as fireweed, is a common sight on disturbed ground, including dug vegetable beds. It grows natively across most of the northern hemisphere and can be a serious weed to combat in the vegetable garden.

It is commonly found in just about any area, though it likes to colonize new areas, particularly those damaged by fire. The plant produces seeds with fluffy, cottony parachutes that allow the seeds to blow a long distance. As a single plant can produce up to 80,000 seeds, it can quickly spread and take over a patch of ground.

In North America, it is commonly referred to as fireweed because the heat from fires help to germinate the seeds. It is also one of the first plants to appear after an area has been devastated by forest fires. In England, it was called bombweed as it was the first plant to appear after areas of the country were bombed during World War II.

The plant will grow up to 5 feet/1.5m and produces long spikes of pink/purple flowers from June through to September. When it has finished flowering, it produces seed capsules that split to set the fluffy seeds free. While it is an annual plant, it produces a lot of seeds that will spread over quite a distance. It has long, branched roots that can produce new shoots, helping the plant to spread.

Gardening Uses

Rosebay willowherb is not cultivated or desired in a garden due to the fact it spreads very rapidly and easily. It should be removed as soon as possible and composted, though if it has gone to seed, destroy the plants instead.

Culinary Uses

The young shoots can be cooked and eaten like asparagus, served with lemon juice and butter. As the plant ages, the leaves become very bitter, but the young leaves work well in salads. The inner part of the stems can be removed and used to thicken stews or soups while the flowers look great on a salad.

In Russia, rosebay willowherb has been fermented to make a herbal tea known as "Ivan Chai" across the rest of Europe. While it is still drunk in some parts of Russia, it has mostly been replaced by black tea now.

The leaves, shoots and roots are all edible and this plant contains high levels of vitamin A and C.

Fireweed is an excellent source of nectar and American beekeepers are known to follow loggers with their hives so the bees can feast on this plant as it sprouts up where the trees are felled. Fireweed honey has a light color and is said to have a good flavor. This honey is particularly popular in Alaska.

Be aware that this plant does contain tannins which could aggravate conditions such as anaemia, gastric ulcers, constipation and inflammatory conditions.

Rosebay Willowherb Cordial
The flowers make a delicious, bright pink cordial, using a method similar to that of elderflower cordial. This cordial will last for several weeks in your refrigerator. When collecting the flowers, try to minimize the amount of green parts you collect as these will make the cordial a bit bitter. This recipe will make about 3½ pints/2 litres of cordial.

Ingredients:
- ½ carrier bag of rosebay willowherb flowers
- 2.2lbs/1kg superfine (caster) sugar
- 2½ pints/1.5 litres water
- 3 unwaxed lemons (sliced)
- 2 unwaxed oranges (sliced)
- 1¼oz/35g citric acid

Method:
1. Shake the flowers carefully to remove dirt and bugs
2. Boil the water in a large pan
3. Once boiling, add the lemons, oranges, citric acid and flowers
4. Stir well, remove from the heat and cover with a tea towel

5. Leave to cool and infuse overnight
6. Strain the liquid through cheesecloth/muslin to remove all the solids, then return to the pan
7. Add the sugar and boil for 5 minutes
8. While still boiling hot, pour into sterilized bottles and seal

Medicinal Uses

In the UK, there are few records of this plant being used as a medicine, but it was used throughout the rest of Europe and across America. Fireweed is used to treat skin complaints, stomach disorders, asthma and whooping cough. The plant has anti-inflammatory properties, stops bleeding and is astringent. It is traditionally used to treat diarrhoea and other digestive problems.

Folklore, Myths and Legends

The seeds make an excellent tinder for lighting fires and the hairs from the seeds have been used as a clothing fiber in the past. After the Great Fire of London in 1666, rosebay willowherb grew in the areas destroyed by the flower and gained its nickname of "London's Ruin".

Self-Heal

Self-heal, *Prunella vulgaris*, is a low to the ground plant that is particularly fond of lawns and difficult to get with a lawnmower. When flowering, it is popular with both bees and butterflies and is edible. As its name suggests, it was a popular medicinal herb in the past that was used to treat a variety of ailments.

This is a perennial plant that will grow from between 4-20"/10-50cm tall with a short rhizome or root crown. It prefers damp soils, though will tolerate drier conditions. The stems and flowers are used to make an olive green dye.

The flowers are tubular in shape and around ½"/1cm long with two lips. The top lip acts as a hood and is light purple. The lower lip is fringed and whiter. The flowers appear from mid to later summer and will remain in bloom for a couple of months before producing four very small seeds.

Self-heal is found across most of the world where it loves to grow in disturbed ground. It can be found almost anywhere from by rivers and lakes to meadows, woodland borders, empty fields and more.

Gardening Uses
Outside of the medicinal garden, self-heal is not commonly grown in gardens these days. It can be composted, though like most plants, it is best to remove the seeds first.

Culinary Uses
The leaves and flowers contain high levels of beneficial antioxidants. Self-heal has been used for thousands of years as a medicine. The raw leaves have a very subtle, bitter taste. It is a good pot herb, but many of the beneficial nutrients are lost in cooking. The leaves can be added to a salad and eaten raw, added to mashed potatoes or put in a soup or stew.

Medicinal Uses
The leaves and stems have antibacterial, astringent and diuretic properties, as well as containing plenty of antioxidants. It can also help reduce blood pressure and reduce blood in urine. The flower spikes were used to restore and protect the liver. It is also used as a gallbladder tonic to help heal complaints of this organ.

Self-heal is commonly taken as a tea, using fresh or

dried leaves. It can be drunk hot or cold.

Self-Heal Skin Cream
This is a simple skin cream that nourishes your skin while protecting it from environmental damage. This recipe makes about 1 cup of cream and takes about 24 hours to make.

Ingredients:
- 1 cup self-heal flowers and leaves (dried)
- ½ cup grapeseed oil
- 4 tablespoons argan oil
- 3 tablespoons dried rosemary
- 1 teaspoon vitamin E oil
- 10 drops frankincense essential oil
- 10 drops lavender essential oil

Method:
1. Put the argan and grapeseed oil into a double boiler together with the rosemary and self-heal
2. Heat until the oil is warm to the touch and leave for 8 hours on this low heat, stirring every hour or two
3. After 8 hours, remove from the heat, cover and leave overnight
4. The next day, heat the oil again until it is warm to the touch
5. Leave for 20 minutes on this low heat
6. Remove from the heat and leave for 10 minutes to cool
7. Use cheesecloth or muslin to strain the oil, squeezing it to get as much as possible through
8. Add the essential oils and vitamin E and stir well
9. Pour into amber bottles or jars and store in a cool, dark location

Folklore, Myths and Legends

Self-heal is used spiritually to give strength to people suffering from long-term illnesses. It is used in healing magic and often added to incense or made into an infused oil used to anoint candles or objects.

According to legend, the druids harvested self-heal at night during the dark phase of the moon, ideally when the Dog Star was rising. It was meant to be dug up using the druid's sickle, then held up with the left hand while the druid gave thanks for the plant. Then, the plant was separated into stems, leaves and flowers ready for drying.

SHEPHERD'S PURSE

Shepherd's purse, *Capsella bursa-pastoris*, is known as lady's purse in some areas and is one of the earliest greens to appear in the wild in spring. It is known by all sorts of names including witch's pouch, St James' weed, mother's heart, blind weed and cocowort.

The leaves are very good in salads or they can be cooked as greens before the flower stalks appear. As the plant flowers, the larger, basal leaves often die back, leaving smaller leaves on the stem. While you can eat these, they tend to get a bit tough, harder to gather and have a much stronger flavor.

This plant is a member of the mustard family, distinguishable by its purse shaped seedpods. The basal leaves are typically hairy and will grow to about 4"/10cm long. The flowers look similar to wild mustard, but are much smaller, about 3-8mm across and white in color. The flowers appear anytime from early spring through to late fall. Shepherd's purse can grow up to 2 feet/60cm tall, but is more commonly around 8-12"/20-30cm tall.

Shepherd's purse originated from Europe, but has spread to most of the rest of the world. It is commonly found in cultivated soil and can be found in gardens, waste areas, grain fields or roadsides.

Gardening Uses

Shepherd's purse is not typically grown in the garden, usually being foraged from the wild. If found in your garden, it can be composted.

Culinary Uses

The leave can be cooked or eaten raw, when they contain more nutrients. The leaves are best used before the plant flowers and become more peppery as the plant ages. The leaves can be used instead of cabbage or cress in any recipe.

Typically, you can find shepherd's purse outdoors most of the year, but it can be dried and stored. The flowering shoots are edible, as are the seeds, which are great on a salad. The root is also edible and when dried and ground, can be used as a substitute for ginger.

Shepherd's Purse Tofu Soup
This dish is popular in China and shepherd's purse can be found at some Chinese grocery stores. This recipe serves 6 people and takes around 25 minutes to make.

Ingredients:
- 8oz/225g shepherd's purse (finely chopped)
- 7oz/200g silken tofu (cut into ½" cubes)
- 4 cups vegetable/chicken stock
- ¼ cup cornstarch mixed with ¼ cup water
- 3 egg whites
- 1½ teaspoons salt
- 1 teaspoon sesame oil
- ¼ teaspoon ground white pepper

Method:
1. Heat the stock in a wok or medium sized pot
2. Add the sesame oil, salt and white pepper and bring to a slow simmer
3. Give the cornstarch mixture a stir then drizzle into the soup while stirring constantly (reduce the heat slightly and keep the soup moving to prevent the cornstarch from clumping up)
4. Simmer for a minute on a low heat then add the shepherd's purse, stirring gently
5. Add the tofu and stir carefully to avoid breaking up the tofu
6. Simmer for a further 2-4 minutes to thicken, stirring occasionally
7. Beat the egg whites for around 10 seconds and pour slowly into the soup, stirring constantly
8. Increase the heat to a simmer, taste and season if required

9.   Serve immediately

Medicinal Uses

The flowers and leaves can be dried and used as a tea, which is beneficial to the kidneys and can help to stop haemorrhaging, which it was used for in World War I. The cold tea can be put onto a cotton bud and used to stop a nosebleed. It is commonly used both internally and externally to stop bleeding.

The Native Americans used shepherd's purse to kill intestinal worms, ease stomach cramps and dysentery and as a lotion to heal poison ivy stings. The famous herbalist Culpeper recommends the juice of this plant as a cure for tinnitus and earache.

Folklore, Myths and Legends

In the past, shepherd's purse was used as a charm to protect from bleeding. The seeds were made into an amulet for teething children. According to tradition, eating the seeds of the first three of these plants you see protects you against diseases for the rest of the year.

The Japanese have a tradition where shepherd's purse is mixed with rice and barley to make a gruel which is eaten every year on January 7th.

Shepherd's purse has a long history of association with humans. Archeologists found shepherd's purse seeds when excavating the Catal Huyuk site in Turkey which dated back to around 5950 BCE.

Both the Romans and Greeks used shepherd's purse as a medicine, and it remained in favor through to the Middle Ages. In 1615, a book written by Gervase Markham called "The English Housewife" had a recipe to treat dysentery which used shepherd's purse.

The leaves were sold as greens in Philadelphia and affected cow's milk, tainting the flavor. Interesting, shepherd's purse is used to treat diarrhea in calves which is nowadays called scours.

A Gardener's Guide To Weeds

WOOD SORREL

Wood sorrel, *Oxalis stricta*, is a wild, edible weed found across Europe and North America. The flowers are used to make yellow, orange and reddish brown dyes. The plant is high in oxalic acid, hence its Latin name. Many people will refer to this plant as oxalis, which means sour.

The leaves of wood sorrel look very similar to the shamrock. There are several varieties of sorrel, though wood sorrel is distinctive as the seed pods bend upwards sharply on their stalks.

The yellow flowers have five petals and are about ½"/1cm across. Typically, oxalis flowers from May through to October. The leaves are smooth and divided into three heart-shaped leaflets, each with a center crease and are usually green, but can be brownish red or have a purple tinge to them. Wood sorrel actually folds its leaves up at night or when under stress, such as growing in full sun. This plant will grow from 4-14"/10-35cm tall.

Oxalis can be found growing in a lot of different places, but prefers partial shade and moist soil. It is common on forest floors or in the shade of fences or trees in the garden.

Gardening Uses
Oxalis is not typically grown in a garden, but will often crop up as a weed. It can be harvested and eaten or composted.

Culinary Uses
People who have gout, arthritis, rheumatism, kidney stones and hyperacidity should avoid any plants that are high in oxalic acid. It is not considered a problem for anyone else when consumed in moderation and as part of a varied diet.

Wood sorrel is very refreshing to eat and acts as a thirst quencher. The leaves, flowers and immature seed pods are edible and have a mildly sour taste, similar to lemons. They can be used in salads, soups and sauces. Wood sorrel tea is cooled and sweetened with honey makes a refreshing drink.

Wood Sorrel Soup

This is a great recipe for soup that has a slightly tangy taste. It serves 4 people and takes about 20 minutes to make.

Ingredients:
- 4-6 cups of wood sorrel (packed)
- ½ cup cream
- ½ cup shallots or onions (finely chopped)
- 2.2 pints/1 litre vegetable stock
- 3 tablespoons unsalted butter
- Pinch of salt

Method:
1. Melt the butter in a large pan and sauté the onions on a medium-low heat
2. Add the stock to the pan and bring to a simmer
3. Reduce the heat to medium, add the sorrel together with a punch of salt and stir well
4. Once the sorrel has wilted, reduce the heat to low
5. Cover, and cook for a further 10 minutes, stirring occasionally
6. Whisk in the cream and simmer on a very low heat for 5 minutes
7. Serve immediately, or cool and serve cold

Medicinal Uses

Wood sorrel is used topically to cool the skin and internally as a diuretic and to soothe the stomach. It is also used to treat fevers, urinary tract infections, sore throats, nausea, scurvy and mouth sores.

A decoction is made from the leaves and taken to treat a fever. It helps to reduce the fever and quench thirst. It is used as a blood cleanser and strengthens the stomach plus helps the appetite.

Folklore, Myths and Legends

In the time of Henry VIII in England, wood sorrel was a very popular pot herb. However, once French Sorrel was introduced, with larger, more succulent leaves, it fell out of favor.

The veins of the flowers are, according to tradition, the mark of Jesus Christ's blood. Wood sorrel is common in crucifixion scenes painted in the 15th century by artists such as Fra Angelico. In Dorset, England, it is known as the "Alleluiah plant" as it flowers between Easter and Whitsun when psalms are sung that end in Alleluiah. Wood sorrel is one of the plants that makes a claim to being the Shamrock that St. Patrick of Ireland used to explain the doctrine of the Holy Trinity.

YARROW

Common yarrow, *Achillea millefolium*, is a mat forming perennial that spreads through rhizomes and is considered by many to be an aggressive weed. It is native to Europe and Asia and has since been introduced to North American where it has become naturalized. It is also found in Australia, South America and Africa. The Achillea in the name refers to the Greek hero Achilles who used the plant in the Trojan Wars to stop bleeding and heal the wounds of his soldiers.

Yarrow leaves are very fern-like and have a distinctive smell. The flowers are dense, flat compound corymbs that bloom throughout the summer months. It is very popular with hoverflies, which are beneficial insects for the garden as they eat pests and bees. Yarrow will grow anywhere from 1-4 feet/30-100cm tall.

Common yarrow likes to grow in sunny areas with thin,

sandy soils, though it will tolerate partial sun. It is common on roadsides, fields, waste ground and even lawns.

Gardening Uses

Yarrow is not commonly grown in the garden, though there are ornamental versions of this plant available with different colored flowers ranging from red to pink to yellow and even bicolor pastels. Yarrow is often found growing wild in the garden and is easy to remove when caught young and then composted. It can be very beneficial in a wild patch of your garden to attract hoverflies and beneficial insects.

Culinary Uses

The leaves are eaten raw or cooked and have a bitter flavor, but they work well in a mixed salad. They are best eaten when young. The leaves can also be used as a substitute for hops in beer making. While this plant is good for you, it is recommended that you do not eat too much of it. The leaves and flowers can be made into a beneficial herbal tea.

Yarrow Omelette
This recipe serves two people and takes around 10 minutes to make. It is very easy to make and is a great breakfast or lunch.

Ingredients:
- 6 eggs
- ¼ cup yarrow (finely chopped)
- 1 small onion (finely chopped)
- Salt and pepper to taste

Method:
1. Beat the eggs in a bowl
2. Add the yarrow and onion, and mix well
3. Cook the omelette how you like it and enjoy

Medicinal Uses

Yarrow has a lot of medicinal uses and is the subject of medical research at the present moment. Researchers at the University of Vienna showed that it can sooth irritable bowel syndrome due to its antispasmodic effects, more at https://www.ncbi.nlm.nih.gov/pubmed/17009839/.

Herbalists use yarrow to lower blood pressure and improve blood circulation.

Of course, the most famous use of yarrow is that it has antimicrobial and styptic properties, meaning it is ideal for stopping bleeding when applied directly to a wound. It also helps to prevent infection to a wound. It can be used as a wash, soak or poultice on a wound and was used as recently as World War II in the field to treat injuries.

If you have toothache, chew a yarrow leaf as it has analgesic properties that will numb the affected area. It can also help alleviate the symptoms of colds and flu. A yarrow mouthwash will help to reduce gum inflammation.

Folklore, Myths and Legends

Yarrow has a very long association with humans and was found, together with other medicinal herbs, in a burial site in Iraq dating from around 60,000BC. It is used in Ayurvedic and Native American medicine. It is also used in Chinese medicine and, famously, is the material from which I-Ching sticks are made from, which is a Chinese divination system.

In Hungary, yarrow is said to help give women going through the menopause strength and energy. In England, yarrow leaves were put inside handkerchiefs and held to the nose keep away colds and flu.

In the 1800's and early 1900's, girls used to go out into a yarrow field under the light of the moon, close their eyes and pick some yarrow. This was taken home and if it was still wet in the morning, their boyfriends would start taking an interest in them very soon.

ENDNOTE

Gardener's hate weeds. It is bred into us and what we are meant to do, but a weed is purely a misplaced plant. Funnily enough, many plants we consider weeds today are ancestors or related to plants we cherish and toil every year to grow.

As our palates have changed over the centuries and farming has become more intensive, humans have bred new varieties of plants that are more productive, more reliable and taste better, usually sweeter. Many of the weeds that we used to eat are quite bitter compared to today's vegetables, but most people nowadays are not very keen on bitter tastes.

What surprised me the most in researching this book was finding out how many of the weeds I regularly dig up are edible and beneficial! These are now being dried and stored for use in tea and as herbs, and some have even made their way into meals, though don't tell the rest of my family! Clover, chickweed, nettles and more grow freely in my vegetable gardens and now I can make use of these, which gives me a sense of satisfaction.

Remember that when you are foraging for these weeds, try to gather them away from roads just to minimize the amount of pollution on them. So many of these weeds are freely available and grow in abundance in the wild.

I also discovered that even the dreaded Japanese knotweed has some uses. The young shoots can be eaten like rhubarb and made into a tasty jam. However, this is not something you want to encourage into your garden and in most countries it is illegal to remove it and transport it to another area.

It isn't just weeds that are edible, so many trees and shrubs produce leaves and fruit that are good to eat. The blackthorn, or sloe, produces berries prized for making sloe gin (if you've never had it, try making it as it is amazing). Its cousin, whitethorn or hawthorn, has a multitude of uses. The young leaves can be eaten raw and have a delicious nutty taste, known as 'bread and cheese' to many foragers. The flowers make a delicate white wine and the berries make a red wine, but are also used medicinally to treat heart conditions.

There is so much in the world around us that can benefit us medicinally and in the kitchen, but we are conditioned to be blinkered from it as our food comes in neat plastic packets from the supermarket.

The next time you are out for a walk, wherever you are. Look down at the ground and see what weeds are growing around you. You will be surprised how many of these weeds are freely available quite close to your home or in your local park. Nature is truly abundant, and discovering what weeds can do for you, is absolutely fascinating. There are so many beneficial plants, not just for eating, but they can be used for herbal medicine and for beauty treatments. Learning all about them is a great way to become more in touch with nature and make use of the weeds you regularly remove from your garden.

ABOUT JASON

Jason has been a keen gardener for over twenty years, having taken on numerous weed infested patches and turned them s.

One of his first gardening experiences was digging over a 400 square foot garden in its entirety and turning it into a vegetable garden, much to the delight of his neighbors who all got free vegetables! It was through this experience that he discovered his love of gardening and started to

155

learn more and more about the subject.

His first encounter with a greenhouse resulted in a tomato infested greenhouse but he soon learnt how to make the most of a greenhouse and now grows a wide variety of plants from grapes to squashes to tomatoes and more.

He is passionate about helping people learn to grow their own fresh produce and enjoy the many benefits that come with it, from the exercise of gardening to the nutrition of freshly picked produce. He often says that when you've tasted a freshly picked tomato you'll never want to buy another one from a store again!

Jason is also very active in the personal development community, having written books on self-help, including subjects such as motivation and confidence. He has also recorded over 80 hypnosis programs, being a fully qualified clinical hypnotist which he sells from his website www.MusicForChange.com.

He hopes that this book has been a pleasure for you to read and that you have learned a lot about the subject and welcomes your feedback either directly or through an Amazon review. This feedback is used to improve his books and provide better quality information for his readers.

Jason also loves to grow giant and unusual vegetables and is still planning on breaking the 400lb barrier with a giant pumpkin. He hopes that with his new allotment plot he'll be able to grow even more exciting vegetables to share with his readers.

OTHER BOOKS BY JASON

Please check out my other gardening books on Amazon, available in Kindle and paperback.

Berry Gardening – The Complete Guide to Berry Gardening from Gooseberries to Boysenberries and More
Who doesn't love fresh berries? Find out how you can grow many of the popular berries at home such as marionberries and blackberries and some of the more unusual like honeyberries and goji berries. A step by step guide to growing your own berries including pruning, propagating and more. Discover how you can grow a wide variety of berries at home in your garden or on your balcony.

Canning and Preserving at Home – A Complete Guide to Canning, Preserving and Storing Your Produce
A complete guide to storing your home-grown fruits and vegetables. Learn everything from how to freeze your produce to canning, making jams, jellies, and chutneys to dehydrating and more. Everything you need to know about storing your fresh produce, including some unusual methods of storage, some of which will encourage children to eat fresh fruit!

Companion Planting Secrets – Organic Gardening to Deter Pests and Increase Yield

Learn the secrets of natural and organic pest control with companion planting. This is a great way to increase your yield, produce better quality plants and work in harmony with nature. By attracting beneficial insects to your garden, you can naturally keep down harmful pests and reduce the damage they cause. You probably grow many of these companion plants already, but by repositioning them, you can reap the many benefits of this natural method of gardening.

Container Gardening - Growing Vegetables, Herbs & Flowers in Containers

A step by step guide showing you how to create your very own container garden. Whether you have no garden, little space or you want to grow specific plants, this book guides you through everything you need to know about planting a container garden from the different types of pots, to which plants thrive in containers to handy tips helping you avoid the common mistakes people make with containers.

Cooking with Zucchini - Delicious Recipes, Preserves and More With Courgettes: How To Deal With A Glut Of Zucchini And Love It!

Getting too many zucchinis from your plants? This book teaches you how to grow your own courgettes at home as well as showing you the many different varieties you could grow. Packed full of delicious recipes, you will learn everything from the famous zucchini chocolate cake to delicious main courses, snacks, and Paleo diet friendly raw recipes. The must have guide for anyone dealing with a glut of zucchini.

Greenhouse Gardening - A Beginners Guide to Growing Fruit and Vegetables All Year Round

A complete, step by step guide to owning your own greenhouse. Learn everything you need to know from sourcing greenhouses to building foundations to ensuring it survives high winds. This handy guide will teach you everything you need to know to grow a wide range of plants in your greenhouse, including tomatoes, chilies, squashes, zucchini and much more. Find out how you can benefit from a greenhouse today, they are more fun and less work than you might think!

Growing Brassicas – Growing Cruciferous Vegetables from Broccoli to Mooli to Wasabi and More

Brassicas are renowned for their health benefits and are packed full of vitamins. They are easy to grow at home, but beset by problems. Find out how you can grow these amazing vegetables at home, including the incredibly beneficial plants broccoli and maca. Includes step by step growing guides plus delicious recipes for every recipe!

Growing Chilies – A Beginners Guide to Growing, Using & Surviving Chilies

Ever wanted to grow super-hot chilies? Or maybe you just want to grow your own chilies to add some flavour to your food? This book is your complete, step-by-step guide to growing chilies at home. With topics from selecting varieties to how to germinate seeds, you will learn everything you need to know to grow chilies successfully, even the notoriously difficult to grow varieties such as Carolina Reaper. With recipes for sauces, meals and making your own chili powder, you'll find everything you need to know to grow your own chili plants

Growing Fruit: The Complete Guide to Growing Fruit at Home

This is a complete guide to growing fruit from apricots to walnuts and everything in between. You will learn how to choose fruit plants, how to grow and care for them, how to store and preserve the fruit and much more. With recipes, advice, and tips this is the perfect book for anyone who wants to learn more about growing fruit at home, whether beginner or experienced gardener.

Growing Garlic – A Complete Guide to Growing, Harvesting & Using Garlic

Everything you need to know to grow this popular plant. Whether you are growing normal garlic or elephant garlic for cooking or health, you will find this book contains all the information you need. Traditionally a difficult crop to grow with a long growing season, you'll learn the exact conditions garlic needs, how to avoid the common problems people encounter and how to store your garlic for use all year round. A complete, step-by-step guide showing you precisely how to grow garlic at home.

Growing Herbs – A Beginners Guide To Growing, Using, Harvesting and Storing Herbs

A comprehensive guide to growing herbs at home, detailing 49 different herbs. Learn everything you need to know to grow these herbs from their preferred soil conditions to how to harvest and propagate them and more. Including recipes for health and beauty plus delicious dishes to make in your kitchen. This step-by-step guide is designed to teach you all about growing herbs at home, from a few herbs in containers to a fully-fledged herb garden. An indispensible guide to growing and using herbs.

Growing Giant Pumpkins – How to Grow Massive Pumpkins at Home

A complete step by step guide detailing everything you need to know to produce pumpkins weighing hundreds of pounds, if not edging into the thousands! Anyone can grow giant pumpkins at home, and this book gives you the insider secrets of the giant pumpkin growers showing you how to avoid the mistakes people commonly make when trying to grow a giant pumpkin. This is a complete guide detailing everything from preparing the soil to getting the right seeds to germinating the seeds and caring for your pumpkins.

Growing Lavender: Growing, Using, Cooking and Healing with Lavender

A complete guide to growing and using this beautiful plant. Find out about the hundreds of different varieties of lavender and how you can grow this bee friendly plant at home. With hundreds of uses in crafts, cooking and healing, this plant has a long history of association with humans. Discover today how you can grow lavender at home and enjoy this amazing herb.

Growing Tomatoes: Your Guide to Growing Delicious Tomatoes at Home

This is the definitive guide to growing delicious and fresh tomatoes at home. Teaching you everything from selecting seeds to planting and caring for your tomatoes as well as diagnosing problems this is the ideal book for anyone who wants to grow tomatoes at home. A comprehensive must have guide.

How to Compost – Turn Your Waste into Brown Gold

This is a complete step by step guide to making your own compost at home. Vital to any gardener, this book will explain everything from setting up your compost heap to how to ensure you get fresh compost in just a few weeks. A must have handbook for any gardener who wants their plants to benefit from home-made compost.

How to Grow Potatoes - The Guide To Choosing, Planting and Growing in Containers Or the Ground

Learn everything you need to know about growing potatoes at home. Discover the wide variety of potatoes you can grow, many delicious varieties you will never see in the shops. Find out the best way to grow potatoes at home, how to protect your plants from the many pests and diseases and how to store your harvest so you can enjoy fresh potatoes over winter. A complete step by step guide telling you everything you need to know to grow potatoes at home successfully.

Hydroponics: A Beginners Guide to Growing Food without Soil

Hydroponics is growing plants without soil, which is a fantastic idea for indoor gardens. It is surprisingly easy to set up, once you know what you are doing and is significantly more productive and quicker than growing in soil. This book will tell you everything you need to know to get started growing flowers, vegetables and fruit hydroponically at home.

Indoor Gardening for Beginners: The Complete Guide to Growing Herbs, Flowers, Vegetables and Fruits in Your House

Discover how you can grow a wide variety of plants in your home. Whether you want to grow herbs for cooking, vegetables or a decorative plant display, this book tells you everything you need to know. Learn which plants to keep in your home to purify the air and remove harmful chemicals and how to successfully grow plants from cacti to flowers to carnivorous plants.

Keeping Chickens for Beginners – Keeping Backyard Chickens from Coops to Feeding to Care and More
Chickens are becoming very popular to keep at home, but it isn't something you should leap into without the right information. This book guides you through everything you need to know to keep chickens from decided what breed to what coop to how to feed them, look after them and keep your chickens healthy and producing eggs. This is your complete guide to owning chickens, with absolutely everything you need to know to get started and successfully keep chickens at home.

Raised Bed Gardening – A Guide to Growing Vegetables In Raised Beds
Learn why raised beds are such an efficient and effortless way to garden as you discover the benefits of no-dig gardening, denser planting and less bending, ideal for anyone who hates weeding or suffers from back pain. You will learn everything you need to know to build your own raised beds, plant them and ensure they are highly productive.

Vertical Gardening: Maximum Productivity, Minimum Space
This is an exciting form of gardening allows you to grow large amounts of fruit and vegetables in small areas, maximizing your use of space. Whether you have a large garden, an allotment or just a small balcony, you will be able to grow more delicious fresh produce. Find out how I grew over 70 strawberry plants in just three feet of ground space and more in this detailed guide.

Worm Farming: Creating Compost at Home with Vermiculture

Learn about this amazing way of producing high-quality compost at home by recycling your kitchen waste. Worms break it down and produce a sought after, highly nutritious compost that your plants will thrive in. No matter how big your garden you will be able to create your own worm farm and compost using the techniques in this step-by-step guide. Learn how to start worm farming and producing your own high-quality compost at home.

WANT MORE INSPIRING GARDENING IDEAS?

This book is part of the Inspiring Gardening Ideas series. Bringing you the best books anywhere on how to get the most from your garden or allotment.

You can find out about more wonderful books just like this one at: www.OwningAnAllotment.com

Follow me for gardening tips, advice and an allotment diary at www.YouTube.com/OwningAnAllotment. Join me on Facebook for regular updates and discussions at www.Facebook.com/OwningAnAllotment.

Find me on Instagram and Twitter as @allotmentowner where I post regular updates, offers and gardening news. Follow me today and let's catch up in person!

Thank you for reading!

Jason Johns